Only The BEST ON SUCCESS

Great ideas for improving your life and your business from some of America's top speakers, trainers, consultants, and authors.

SHEP HYKEN • SUE HERSHKOWITZ • ROGER CRAWFORD • LISA FORD
LARRY WINGET • SCOTT FRIEDMAN • WILLIE JOLLEY • SCOTT MCKAIN
CHRIS CLARKE-EPSTEIN • MARK SANBORN • KEITH HARRELL

ONLY THE BEST

ON

SUCCESS

compiled by
Larry Winget

Copyright © MCMXCV

Printed in the United States Of America.

Cover design and layout by Ad Graphics, Tulsa, Oklahoma.

Library of congress Catalog Number: 95-61934

ISBN:1-881342-10-7

Published by:

Win Publications!
a subsidiary of Win Seminars!, Inc.
P. O. Box 700485
Tulsa, Oklahoma 74170
918 745-6606

Addtional copies of
Only The Best On Success
can be obtained from any of the authors by calling their individual number as listed with their chapter.

Quantity discounts are available.

All of the authors represented in
Only The Best On Success
are members of the
National Speakers Association.

If you have an upcoming meeting and need a great speaker or even several great speakers then this book represents some of the finest in the business. Any of them would do an excellent job presenting an informative, entertaining keynote or seminar.

Please contact any speaker to recieve a full packet of materials explaining their speaking services and other products that may be available.

CONTENTS

1

Only The BEST

YOU ARE THE MAGIC!

BY

SHEP HYKEN

SUCCESS

You Are The Magic!

Shep Hyken

There are so many ways to be successful. There are business strategies, motivational strategies, etc. *You Are the Magic* is a motivational title, but I promise to deliver to you information that will bring you more success and happiness in your business and personal lives!

A few years ago I interviewed a number of successful people. These people were really good at what they did. They may or may not have been financially successful, but everyone had success in either their business or personal lives. They were asked a number of questions about what made them successful. There were many answers, but some happened to come up again and again. All of these common answers tied into the relationship that these people had with other people - either how they treated others or how others perceived them to be.

Building and sustaining a relationship with a person is what makes business and personal relationships successful. Anyone can do it, once you know the secrets. And, you are about to learn the secrets to achieving this success.

First, you need to understand what goes into making the success. You need to learn and manage just a few key principles, and you will have what it takes. You will have the magic!

What you are about to learn, you already know. It is common sense. There are five key points you have to know and understand, but that is not the real secret. The real secret is knowing how to use them together. Using just one or two of these may give you an edge, but combining them all is the real secret.

So let's head straight into what it takes to have and be the MAGIC!

Management of the First Impression

Management of the first impression does not mean making a good impression the first time you meet someone. It means managing the first impression of *every* meeting with *anyone*. It may be the first time or the five millionth time you are seeing or talking to someone. For every interaction, make the first reaction someone has when they see or talk to you a positive one. This means the way you greet people, the way you answer the phone, the way you look people in the eye, shake their hand, etc. Are you always on time or usually late? Do you dress for success? By the way, that doesn't always mean wearing a suit or a dress. It simply means dressing appropriately. What kind of reaction does a spouse, significant other or a friend have when they see you after work? Do you bring home an attitude that other people don't want to be around?

There is an old expression that says you can't judge a book by its cover. That may be great advice for you to follow, but don't count on other people accepting it. You need every edge you can get, so take control. It is very simple to manage that first impression. By managing every initial contact you can create a positive first impression, and thereby set the tone for what is to follow.

Acknowledgment of Others

Dale Carnage once said, *"Remember that a man's name is, to him, is the sweetest and most important sound in any language."*

What Mr. Carnage was trying to say is that acknowledgment and recognition are very special to that person. They are a very important key to the success of building a relationship with someone. It can be as simple as using a person's name, but you can go much further. Acknowledge people by sending a note or making a phone call. This is very simple, but is an incredibly powerful tool if used correctly. Use it with your customers, the people you work with, friends, family and loved ones.

For customers you may send a thank you note. Or, try sending a thank you note to someone you work with, thanking them for doing a great job. A customer will think a note is a nice touch, but someone you work with will be surprised and truly appreciate this form of acknowledgment.

We are constantly acknowledging the people we care most about. There are actually "holidays" to acknowledge others. There is Valentines Day, Boss's Day, Secretary's Day, etc. However, to acknowledge people on these days is primarily out of obligation. What do you think would happen if you didn't acknowledge your spouse or "significant other" on Valentine's Day? The rest of the world is doing it, so you had better do it also. In addition to these days of obligation, try doing something special for someone when they don't expect it. That is the powerful way to use this principle.

So send notes and cards, make special phone calls, pat a co-worker on the back and tell your spouse and kids you love them. Acknowledgment is simply making people feel appreciated and recognized for being important to you.

General and Professional Knowledge

Knowledge is another important key to the MAGIC formula. There are two types of knowledge - general and professional.

General knowledge means knowing a little bit about a lot of things. It means knowing what is going on in the world and in your community. It means being well read. General knowledge gives you the ability to communicate with people about their interests, not just yours. You should be able to talk to people about their hobbies, politics, etc. Listen to the news at night and read the newspaper. Expand your mind. Read books. Fiction is great, but mix it up with some nonfiction. Talk about what you are reading. It makes you a more interesting person.

Professional knowledge means you know as much there is to know about your job, your company and the industry you work in. The key is to be up to date with the latest, the greatest and the state of the art. Learn as much as you can. Attend professional seminars. Read literature about the products and services that you and your company sell. Get the literature that your company's competition uses to sell their customers. Read the annual reports from publicly held companies within your industry. Your peers at work and your customers will seek you out as a source of information.

Imagine knowing so much about your business that your customers wouldn't trust anyone except you to answer any questions they might have about their business. There are companies that attempt to position themselves and their employees as the experts. Their customers call them for any questions relating to their products and industry - even if the questions are about the competition. Professional knowledge will give you an incredible edge in your career.

Imagination

Imagination is a tough one to describe. This is not about being creative. In this context you need to use your imagination to be thinking about the other person. In professional and personal relationships you need to have imagination in order to really understand people. In business you may think you know what your customers want, but what they want may be something different. Perhaps it is just a misunderstanding. The same applies in our personal lives.

There is a cute story about a couple driving down the street. They are driving by an ice cream parlor when the woman asks her date, "Would you like some ice cream?" He says, "No" and continues to drive past the ice cream parlor. Actually, she wanted the ice cream and she was only politely asking him to stop. He just didn't get it. He wasn't thinking like her. Otherwise, he would have realized that she wasn't asking him if *he* wanted ice-cream. She was asking him to pull over so *she* could get some. She could have been a little more direct and said, "pull over and let's get some ice cream." If he didn't want any, he wouldn't have to eat any, but at least she would get what she wanted.

This is a classic example of a person not thinking about or like the other person. How may times have you misunderstood someone? One way to overcome this is simply to use imagination and think about what the other people want versus what it is that you think that they want. You don't have to use ESP to read their minds. You simply have to use your imagination and try to start thinking like they do, or at least come up with the right questions to show that you care about what the other person is thinking. It is a simple way of showing people that you care.

Charisma

People like to be around charismatic people. Now, that doesn't mean that you have to jump up and down and always be in a great mood. But, you do need to have an inner enthusiasm. I have seen many corporate executives and politicians make speeches. Some of them are terrible speakers, but they have that charisma. They speak in a dull, almost monotone voice, yet somehow they motivate their audience. The enthusiasm is coming from their hearts. You may not see it in their physical gestures and movement, but you can see it in their eyes.

There was a man who used to teach a seminar with me. He was, without a doubt, one of the most boring speakers ever. When he was younger, he must have had a charisma bypass. Seriously, he would get up in front of the crowd and start his presentation. He would usually lecture for at least four hours. You could tell that the crowd was not happy when he first started. They would start to squirm in their chairs. However, within about fifteen to twenty minutes they would start to relax. The audience would start to soak in all of this man's information. They would start to thirst for his knowledge. And, he was trying to give as much of it to them as he could. Yes, there was the key. He was a terrible speaker, a boring speaker, but he was excited about delivering to his audience some important information. He was an expert, and while he didn't show his charisma on the outside, he had it in his heart. He wanted his audiences to learn and he was going to teach them what they needed to know to be successful - and they knew it.

Be excited about life - about your personal and professional life. You don't always need to be in an incredibly great mood, but you have to at least have an inner enthusiasm. There is an old expression that says, *"Enthusiasm is contagious."* Go a step further and listen to what motivational speaker Danny Cox says. *"If enthusiasm is contagious, then what you have that is not enthusiasm is also contagious."*

So there you have it. Five ways to be the MAGIC! Remember the formula:

- **Management of the first impression**

- **Acknowledgment of others**

- **General and business knowledge**

- **Imagination**

- **Charisma**

It is very easy to put these into use. Take one principle at a time and work on it. For example, spend the next few days working on managing your first impression. Be aware of what you wear, how you greet people, showing up on time, etc. At the end of the day, jot down a few of the times throughout the day when you know you were putting this principle into practice.

After you feel comfortable with managing the first impression, move onto acknowledgment of others. Be conscious of when you are using this principle. After a short while, maybe just a day or so, it should become second nature.

Do the same with the other three. Within a week or two these principles should become second nature and be a part of your life.

Continue to practice these five principles and you will be amazed with the results. Remember, the key is to not just do one or two, but to use all five at the same time. There are times where one of these principles may be more important than another, but all five have to be there. How well you work and get along with other people is important. But, how others think of you can make a difference in your personal success. By using the MAGIC formula you can be yourself, but still use techniques to make you stand out and be noticed.

Remember, you are the MAGIC!

SHEP HYKEN

Shep Hyken, CSP is a speaker and author who has been entertaining audiences with his unique presentation style for 24 years. He has been hailed as one of the top entertainer/magicians working the corporate field. In 1983 he made the transition from entertainer to speaker. Hyken mixes information with entertainment (humor and magic) to create exciting programs for his audiences.

Shep Hyken's most requested programs focus on customer service, internal service, customer relations, and a motivational program titled *"You Are The Magic!"*

Shep Hyken has worked with hundreds of companies and associations ranging from "Fortune 500" size companies to smaller organizations with less than 50 employees. Some of his clients include American Airlines, Anheuser-Busch, AT&T, Fleming Foods, General Motors, Holiday Inn, Kraft, Monsanto, Shell Oil, Standard Oil and many, many more.

OTHER PRODUCTS

Moments of Magic — 158 page book $12.95
A clearly written, easy-to-read, easy to understand guide to customer service. It is for anyone in any job. It is filled with information, techniques and stories that will teach you to deliver excellent service to your internal and outside customers.

Shep Hyken "Live" Customer Service — 55 minute video $49.00
Video of customer service covering topics such as complaining customers, relationship skills, moments of truth, and several other important issues. This was taped in front of a live audience and combines information and entertainment (humor and magic) to create an exciting presentation.

Service: Creating Moments of Magic — 2 videos & workbook $99.00
A video *learning system* with a focus on internal and external customers. The workbook includes exercises that will *personalize* the information to the viewer's day-to-day responsibilities.
Additional workbooks $5.00
Facilitator Guide for above $9.00

Please add $4.00 Shipping & Handling
Call regarding multiple orders

For more information contact:
Shep Hyken
Shepard Presentations
711 Old Ballas Rd., Suite 103
St. Louis, MO 63141
(800) 829-3888
(314) 692-2200
FAX: (314) 692-2222
E Mail: ShepardH@Aol.com

2

Only The BEST

THE FUTURE IS FOR THE OPEN MINDED™

BY

SUE HERSHKOWITZ

SUCCESS

THE FUTURE IS FOR THE OPEN MINDED™

SUE A. HERSHKOWITZ, CSP

Are you old enough to remember the Ed Sullivan Show? If you were a frequent watcher or not, you may remember a man who actually made his living spinning plates. He would take this long metal pole and balance a plate on it, then start the plate spinning. Soon, he would have a dozen or more plates spinning! The audience would watch breathlessly as first a plate on the right would begin to wobble, then one on the left. He'd keep running and keep spinning...

Thinking about that act, the other day, I realized that his spinning plates are really a metaphor for what's going on in our personal and professional lives today! Change, today, is the status quo and the opportunities and challenges it brings can be both frightening and exciting.

It seems there are two choices each of us has: One

choice is to close our eyes really, really tight and hope that when we open them nothing will have changed (not possible!) or that we will have retired (depends how old you were when you were watching the Ed Sullivan show!). The other choice is to open our eyes really wide and look at the new opportunities, the new possibilities change brings.

What do successful people do to balance those plates?

Change the Rules

Years ago when I was teaching junior high school, a young woman named Colleen, would tell me the weirdest things each morning. "Spaghetti, that's what we had for breakfast this morning," she would say. "It was meat loaf this morning...," or maybe, "The roast beef today was great." I did my best to avoid getting into a protracted conversation with her regarding these "stories" and decided I would bring it up with her mother at Open House.

I started with a great report about Colleen and finally, carefully, broached the subject, "There's just one thing I'd like to talk to you about. Colleen tells me she had roast beef, for breakfast and spaghetti and meat loaf. .." Her mother was silent for a moment. "She didn't tell you about my vegetarian lasagna?!" I was convinced they were both loony!

She went on to explain: A few months ago she had become deeply depressed. She had a family - a husband who worked as many hours a day as she did, a teen aged son who went to work directly from school, and Colleen, involved in band, drama and other after school activities. She never saw her family - they never had a time to come together and it was making her miserable and depressed.

In an attempt to work through her illness, she brought the family together and asked for a huge favor. She told them that she had noticed that on most days, no one left the house before 7:20 am. What she was proposing was that she would prepare the family dinner meal for breakfast. She would get up as early as she had to to cook that day's dinner, and she needed the family to agree to be at the dinner table at 7:00 am sharp so they could eat leisurely and talk together. If they would give it a three month trial, she would be happy.

Hoping it would help their mom, they agreed. She said it was terrible, at first. By 8:00 am during those first two weeks everyone had indigestion! Slowly, everyone stopped complaining. She knew she had won them over when one morning she heard her son as he was coming out of the shower yelling, "What's for dinner, ma ... omelle great!"

She changed the rules!

Southwest Airlines is another rule changer. Southwest Airlines began as a small regional carrier. They have never offered their passengers assigned seats. Instead, each person receives a boarding card - first come, first served - and when it's departure time, they yell: "Numbers 1-30 line up." And, pushing and shoving to beat out the next person to avoid that awful middle seat, you do!

Southwest has never served food on their flights - regardless of the duration of the flight. Even a flight from Phoenix to Baltimore, (with intermediary stops in Indianapolis and St. Louis) offers only peanuts and drinks.

Baggage is not interlined on Southwest. If you fly Southwest from Detroit to Los Angeles (with intermediary stops in Chicago Midway, Dallas Love and Phoenix) and want to transfer to Hawaiian Airlines, you must retrieve your own baggage from the Southwest baggage carousel and carry it to Hawaiian for check in.

Can you imagine? Absolutely the longest way from one point to another. Absolutely no frills. Absolutely nothing, but getting you to your destination on time at the least expensive fare.

Now, get this: Three years in a row, Southwest Airlines beat out almost every other major US carrier - including those who pride themselves on RESPECT - in both customer service and customer satisfaction. What's going on here?

Southwest changed the rules. Instead of promising the sun and the moon and the stars, and then failing to deliver, they changed the strategy. They promise the sun and they deliver the sun *and* the moon. The result? Loyalty and delighted customers.

What does it take to change the rules? Opening your eyes to the opportunities around you. Focusing on the things you do well - your personal and professional core competencies - and enhancing them. Understanding that your resiliency - your ability to change the rules, to adapt to change around you, to twist the familiar - is your key to success.

Resiliency

Every billionaire ever interviewed has cited resiliency as a prime ingredient in his or her success. Samuel Walton of Wal-Mart fame, in one of his last interviews, spoke about how fortunate he was at a very young age to discover the power of resiliency. He told the story of working as a clerk in a Montgomery Ward's sporting goods department. In those days, he explained, it wasn't enough for a clerk to simply sell the items - sales help actually had to understand both how products were made and how they were used. (What a concept!!!)

He was on a tour of a pool table manufacturing plant and when he first arrived, to his untrained eye, all the tables looked the same though they were priced quite differently. He learned that the materials may be different, yes, but the real worth, the true value of the pool table lies in the *resiliency* of the cushioning. He said it was as if he was hit with a bolt of lightning. He realized at that moment that his value would be dependent on his ability to be resilient, adaptable, flexible. So will yours and mine.

How can you enhance resiliency?

Twist the Familiar

Begin by twisting the familiar. Ask yourself: What am I doing now that appears to be sacred, that I've been doing for years, and I don't really know why I'm doing it?

Being Jewish, I light Friday night Shabbat candles. The Catholic man I was dating learned that those candles could not be blown out; it was important for them to extinguish themselves. (They stay lit two - three hours.) One Friday night, shortly after we were married, we decided to go to a movie. As we were cleaning up, I noticed, out of the corner of my eye, that he was moving the candles! Intellectually, I understood exactly what he was doing. I lit the candles on the kitchen table which is in line with the front door. Theoretically, as we closed the door behind us on the way to the movie, we could set off a breeze, and the wind would hit the candles with such force that the silver candlesticks my grandmother gave me would be knocked down, the candles would set the wood table on fire and we would come home to a raging fire. Intellectually, I understood. Emotionally, I didn't. I knew those candles weren't to be moved. "Stop," I yelled, "Don't move those candles." He looked like a deer caught in headlights! "Okay, why?" "Why?" (how dare he question!), "Why? I don't know why! I just know you're not supposed to move those candles!" So I called my mother and asked her. "Why?" she asked. "Why? I don't know why...

I just know you're not supposed to move the candles."

And so it goes! What is sacred in your personal or professional life that has no rhyme or reason and you continue to do it anyway? How can you do it differently, better, more meaningfully? Is it time to break it, so you can fix it?

To become more resilient, ask yourself: What are the classic frustrations my customers, my family, that I have, that no one has yet solved? Start thinking outside of the box to solve them.

Here's a riddle: A friend you hadn't seen in years popped into town just when you were selling your laptop computer. He gave you a check for your asking price of $1,000 check. You spent some time together that Saturday afternoon reminiscing and he and you went on your way. Tuesday, you go to your bank to deposit the check. Sorry, you're told, insufficient funds. Because you're friends with the bank manager, she tells you your friend has only $967 in his account in his bank in another state. Oh, and by the way, when she called that bank manager, he said he had a note that your friend was leaving the country.

You're sunk. No laptop... no money ... no friend. How will you get your money? Think about it. How *will* you get the money that is rightfully owed to you? There is no way, with only $967 in the account that the bank can cash the check.

The only way to collect your money is to twist the familiar - to think outside of the box - and deposit $37 into your friend's account!

Think about the challenges the new opportunities are presenting. How can you solve them? What new products, tools, solutions are needed to take care of the way of doing business?

Twist the familiar by thinking through what business you're really in. Ron Pobuda, speaking at the Professional Convention Managers Association, said, "If Sports Illustrated magazine had understood they were in the sports information business and not the publishing business, today we would have the Sports Illustrated channel, not ESPN." What business are you in? Do you sell washing machines or fabric care solutions? Refrigerators or food preservation systems? Seminars or solutions? Develop new products or new ways of communicating those products, create new solutions or unique ways of partnering (and partners) to build tomorrow's solutions.

Become a learning organization

The ability to be adaptable starts with having the confidence that you can change with change. When was the last time you took a college course? Learned a new skill? Did something that was outside of your comfort zone? Alvin Toffler said, "The illiterate of the future are not those who cannot read and write. The illiterate of the future are those who cannot learn, unlearn and relearn."

Set aside fifteen minutes a day as your personal R & D time. The more you learn, the more you earn, today and even more so, in the future.

The Success Factor

There really is only one way to control those spinning plates. Focus today on the future needs of your customers and clients. Start thinking right now, right this very moment, about how you can link your ideas, products and services to the opportunities of continuous change and the challenges of tomorrow.

Eleanor Roosevelt said, "The future belongs to those who believe in the beauty of their dreams." Start dreaming and planning today!

SUE HERSHKOWITZ, CSP

Sue A. Hershkowitz has **spoken before more than three-quarters of a million people** both nationally and internationally during the past 14 years. Her corporate, association and government client list reads like a Who's Who of recognizable names, including: Walt Disney Studios, Marriott Hotels and Resorts, American Express, the US Navy and even the IRS! Sue has presented to associations such as the Young President's Organization, American Heart Association, American Society of Association Executives and has been **asked back by Meeting Professionals International twelve times!**

Sue holds a B.A. in English, a masters degree in Counseling and earned a **fellowship sponsored by the University of California at Berkeley.** Twice elected to the **Board of Directors of the National Speakers Association,** Sue currently serves on both the Executive and Finance committees. In addition, she has served on Meeting Professionals International **Meeting Manager** Editorial Advisory Board and the **Meeting News** Industry Advisory Board.

In 1993, Sue earned her **Certified Speaking Professional** designation. This recognition has been presented to fewer than

300 of the 3,300 National Speakers Association members. The C.S.P. signifies Sue's commitment and dedication to the speaking profession.

Sue's book, P*ower Sales Writing: What Every Sales Person Needs To Know to Turn Prospects Into Buyers!* is the **business building book** of the year! Everyone needs to communicate more powerfully and this book provides specific strategies and training examples to give readers the **definitive edge**.

Sue is known for her **content-rich presentations**, **fresh perspective** and her **energetic, enthusiastic** and **entertaining speaking style**. Her keynotes and workshops provide **practical, immediately usable** tools and techniques focused on empowering attendees to reach their professional and personal potential. Call Sue to jump start your next meeting!

Future Focus
• The Future is for The Open Minded
• Twisting the Familiar: Keys to Success, Profits and Sales
• "Magic Eye" Thinking: See the Possibilities

Customer Service
• Hyperservice™
• Service Doesn't Cost Extra!
• The Banana Peel Factor: How to Keep Your Customers From Slipping Out the Door!

Communications
• Power Writing
• You Think I Said What?
• Dealing with Crazy People - and Getting Results!

For more information on Sue's Keynotes and Intensive Training Workshops, please call 602•996•8864.

OTHER PRODUCTS

Power Sales Writing: What Every Sales Person Needs To Know to Turn Prospects Into Buyers! — 140 pages $15.95
Compel your prospects to read your message. Discover how you can grasp their attention within five seconds and save up to 80% of the time you now spend writing. If you communicate in writing, this book is a must-read.

The Banana Peel Factor: How To Keep Your Customers From Slipping out the Door!
Videotape - 60 Minutes $59.95
Understanding what service factors matter to your customers can make the difference between average service and legendary. This live presentation will keep you laughing as you learn how you can exceed customer expectations for greater loyalty and profits.

The Success Formula: How To Get the Results You Want!
Audiotape - 60 minutes $14.95
What can you do to reach your personal and professional potential? Find out how successful people master change, communicate more persuasively, and position themselves for success.

Dog Tales for the Heart — Approx. 110 pages — Pre-Release Price $15.95
To be released December 1995. A compilation of true stories to warm your heart and inspire your soul. You'll laugh and cry with the sweetness and unconditional love provided by our faithful companions. Real people and regular dogs together for an unbeatable combination of love, motivation and inspiration. Buy a copy for yourself and another to give as a gift. Every dog lover will treasure this book!

Please add $3.95 for postage and handling. Items will be sent two-day mail.

Special Offer
Order Power Sales Writing and The Success Formula and enjoy the customer service video, The Banana Peel Factor, for a 50% saving ($30.00).
Or
Order The Banana Peel Factor and select either Power Sales Writing or The Success Formula as our gift to you.

To order these products or to speak to Sue
about availability for an upcoming meeting, please call:
High Impact Presentations
14826 North 54th Place
Scottsdale, AZ 85254
V. 602-996-8864 • F. 602-996-6667
or
Hershk @ AOL   74117,56 @ Compuserve

3

Only The BEST

Believe Success Is Possible

BY

ROGER CRAWFORD

SUCCESS

Believe Success Is Possible

ROGER CRAWFORD

Believing that success is possible begins with accepting what we cannot change. I was born with a number of physical problems, but fortunately I was gifted with extraordinary parents. Doctors told my mother and father that I would never walk. But in 1984 I ran one and a half miles through downtown San Francisco carrying the Olympic torch, on that part of its journey from Athens, Greece to Los Angeles, California. Running with the torch was a triumphant moment for me. People were leaning out of windows waving American flags and cheering me on as I ran through Union Square, then through Chinatown.

Of course, I've had to accept that there are some things I really can't do. My right arm ends in a thumb without much of a palm. My left hand has a thumb and a pinkie finger. The bottom half of my left leg was amputated when I was five years old so that I could be fitted with an artificial leg, a *prosthesis*. My right foot has three toes. When I was growing up people often called me "handicapped" or "disabled." Today, in the age of political correctness, people call me "physically challenged." (We no longer say someone is short and bald instead he is "vertically challenged" and "his hair is in retreat." A friend of mine says, "I used to have a crew cut, but my crew bailed out.")

My life began to move forward when I accepted that there were some things that I could not change. Early on, I recognized that I would probably never be a concert pianist, a speed typist or a ballet dancer. However, my limitations did not prevent me from becoming a tennis player in high school as well as in college. (By the way, I've played John McEnroe, which was a humbling experience for any tennis player, and one that taught me while a negative attitude guarantees losing, the most positive attitude can't guarantee winning!)

YOUR CHOICES

My eagerness to delve into the subject of optimism started some years ago when a man called and said he would like to meet me. He had seen a newspaper article regarding my tennis career and thought we had something in common. Intrigued, I agreed to get together at a nearby restaurant. He described himself: 6' 2" with a mustache and curly hair.

I arrived early, and when I spotted him coming in the door, I got up and went over to shake his hand. He extended his arm and I realized that his hands were almost identical to mine.

At first, as we talked, I was excited about meeting someone so similar to myself, but older, someone who might share with me some of the wisdom of his life. Instead, what I encountered was someone with a bitter, pessimistic attitude who blamed all of life's disappointments and failures on his anatomy.

I soon recognized that our lives and attitudes couldn't have been more different. Where my parents had insisted on "mainstreaming" me and had turned out to cheer me on at sporting events, his parents kept him sheltered at home, urging him not to overtax himself. They had understandably tried to shield him from life's hardships and pain, but this was the very thing he most resented. He had never held a job for long, and was sure this was because of discrimination—certainly not because he was constantly late, frequently absent, and failed to take any responsibility for his work. I am not saying that his life hadn't been filled with rejection, but when we talked, I heard his words differently because I had similar experiences. His attitude was "the world owes me." And the problem was that most of the world disagreed. He was somewhat angry with me because I did not share his despair. We kept in touch for a number of years and it slowly dawned on me that if, by some miracle, he were suddenly given a perfect body, his unhappiness and lack of success still would not change. He would simply search out some other explanation for his pessimism.

This chance encounter with someone so similar, and yet so different, changed my life. I suddenly understood <u>the quality of our lives is governed by the choices that we make not the circumstances that we face.</u> This is what inspired me to find out why some of us are programmed to make positive choices and some of us aren't.

WHAT IS OPTIMISM?

Optimism is often called *hope* by philosophers, *faith* by clergymen and *hardiness* by the medical profession. It is another way of describing a positive attitude.

First, let me tell you what optimism <u>isn't</u>. Optimism is not a vague sense of well-being or the unsupported illogical belief that somehow everything will turn out all right. It isn't a Pollyanna attitude or wishful thinking, and it doesn't mean ignoring life's realities, while waiting around for nice things to happen. Optimism is not gullibility or blind trust. It isn't trying to draw an inside straight or invest your retirement fund with a fast-talking banana oil salesman. You can combine true optimism with reality, maintaining a healthy skepticism about the potential foibles of your fellow creatures.

Dr. Charles Snyder, a psychologist at the University of Kansas, has done extensive research on the role of optimism in our lives and work. He says, "the notion that everything will turn out all right is not concrete enough and it blurs two key components. Having hope means believing you have both the will and the way to accomplish your goals, whatever they may be."

I feel that authentic optimism must meet certain criteria, <u>will</u> and <u>way</u>, plus the judgment to recognize and evaluate what's happening.

A University of Chicago study of middle and upper level managers concluded that the three most important factors for succeeding under stress were challenge, control and commitment. These three factors parallel my three components of optimism: <u>Recognizing and accepting the situation</u> (challenge). <u>Deciding that you have, or can get the resources to handle it</u> (control). <u>Doing so.</u> (commitment).

I believe that optimism is a conscience choice, a *selective perception* that uses learned skills. We have the power to choose our response to any situation. If you doubt this, consider the average human response to Coue's classic imaginary plank. The French psychotherapist, Emile Coue', demonstrated the power of perception in the early twentieth century with this proposition: take a thick plank a foot wide and 20 feet long. Lay it flat on the ground and ask people to walk the length of it without stepping off. Almost everyone will be able to do so easily. Now place the plank between two church spires several hundred feet in the air and repeat the request. Few will agree to try. The plank is still a foot wide and 20 feet long.

Nothing has changed, except the perception of danger. If we are more likely to fall, it is because we _choose_ to feel fear.

Obviously fear and other strong feelings are highly appropriate and even helpful in certain situations. We are unlikely to feel joyful about a terrible disaster, but nothing can devastate us without our permission. Being challenged is inevitable. Being defeated is optional. When we are derailed by circumstances, it is because we are not focusing on one of the components of optimism, our personal resources. Circumstances can only batter us when we have not defined our lives.

We are products of our choices, not our circumstances. It is not the events that define our lives but how we respond to them. Other people can attempt to control our circumstances but they cannot control our attitudes unless we let them. We invent and create our lives everyday with the choices that we make. Our lives are the products of our attitudes.

There are some things we can try to influence but which ultimately we cannot control: other people's attitudes and actions, weather, passage of time, etc. There are some things we can control: our values, feelings, thoughts, actions, and our _attitudes_ towards other people's attitudes and actions, weather, etc.

Choosing how we view and respond to these events is called *selective perception.* All of us have things in our lives that we realize can't be changed. At this point we have a conscience choice. We can choose to feel frustrated, miserable, angry, depressed, hopeless. Or, we can select an alternative perception. We can intentionally choose to see the unchangeable as a useful tool or a source of amusement, as inspiring, energizing or utterly irrelevant. For example, positive thinking can never change my hands or legs, but it can certainly change how I view my own situation.

YOU ARE WHAT YOU THINK

Your subconscious mind is inherently optimistic. If you doubt this, watch what happens when someone tells a child, "Don't put beans in your ear." Chances are they will soon make a trip to the doctor for bean removal. This is because the subconscious mind does not accept the negative "don't". It concentrates on the rest of the message. Bluebeard told his wife, "Don't open that door," and she opened it. In the War of 1812, Captain James Lawrence told his men, "Don't give up the ship," and they surrendered it.

Messages that are framed with a negative may communicate the opposite of what is intended— "don't drive to fast," "don't forget," or "don't drop that," "don't trip," "don't fail", or "don't despair." Our minds instantly focus on french fries or the potential for fumbling, and ignore the negative qualifier.

The moral is: make positive statements only when you're communicating with yourself or with others. Frame every idea as positively as possible. For example, don't say, "I won't fall below my sales quota this month." Instead say, "I will meet my sales quota this month." Instead of saying, "Don't eat junk food," say, "Eat all those fabulously delicious foods that nourish and nurture the body." Like the old Johnny Mercer/Harold Arlen song says, "Accentuate the positive, eliminate the negative."

As humans, we are only capable of dealing with one thought at a time. Therefore it is impossible to be both optimistic and pessimistic simultaneously. We have to choose, and we become what we think about most. This is called the *principle of dominate thought*.

Richard Bach, in his book <u>Illusions</u> says, "Argue for your limitations and they are yours." Shakespeare has Hamlet say, "For nothing is either good nor bad, but thinking makes it so." Positive words make us strong. Negative words make us weak. Just as we watch what we put into our bodies, we must monitor what we put into our minds.

The religious and political leader, Mohandas Gandhi, who used nonviolence as a tool for social change, knew the importance of positive input. He said, "Keep my words positive because my words become behaviors. Keep my behaviors positive because my behaviors become habits. Keep my habits positive because my habits become my values. Keep my values positive because they become my destiny."

OTHER FOOD FOR THOUGHT

Physically fit people understand the importance of good nutrition. After a strenuous workout they replenish their body with good food. The same is true for people who stay in optimal mental shape. Building optimism requires the careful nourishment. We need the right mental nutrition.

Dr. Denis Waitley says, "The experiences we choose to drive our lives are like the software that drives the hardware." The quality and power can vary tremendously. Early computer programmers had a motto, garbage in - garbage out. You cannot expect quality product without quality ingredients.

Everyone, sometimes in their lives, have felt ugly, stupid and rejected. I certainly have, but my life began to change when I realized what I could control was my _attitude_. Whenever I meet people for the first time and they ask me how I am doing, I always reply "Great!" You may think that is a little disingenuous because no one feels great all the time, but it is all a matter of attitude. My definition of great is if you can wake up in the morning, draw in a breath, you have something to wear, something to eat, and someone to love, then that's a <u>great</u> day. Therefore, up to now, every day of my life has been a great day.

What about people who wake up to misery, to life without health, shelter, food, or people that they love. They could not possibly have anything to be optimistic about, but amazingly many do. Even when optimism consists of a simple statement, "I made it." In the blackest of situations, people often use humor to keep going. Recently I was speaking in Germany and I met a successful young business woman who had grown up under communism. I asked her how she maintained her optimism when her life seemed to hold so few options. She replied, "My father always said, 'Be thankful for what we have, and at least we're not Bulgarians.'"

Now I certainly don't recommend disparaging anyone else to maintain your optimism, but sometimes the knot you hang onto at the end of your rope can be a cynical private joke. Maybe, something like, "At least I'm not in Cleveland." (Before you loyal Clevelanders grab your picket signs, you should know that I'm proud to have grown up in that beautiful city.)

Being thankful for something can be tremendously difficult during challenging times. I often ask people in my audiences to list people or circumstances they are thankful for. Some are, understandably, skeptical, cynical and even embarrassed. How can something so trite and seemingly simplistic make a difference? But I never fail to be astounded at how peoples perspectives and attitudes begin to shift with this simple act. Noticing what we are grateful for sharpens our perceptions and, yes, strengthens our character. When we begin to acknowledge what we have in our lives, we suddenly notice possibilities we've been overlooking. The late Dr. Norman Vincent Peale called this expanded awareness, "the attitude of gratitude." Go get a piece of paper and pencil. If you are a confirmed cynic, your greatest challenge may be persuading yourself to try it, but I guarantee you'll be surprised at the positive results.

Of course there are situations that even the most optimistic person will acknowledge are horrible—war, cruelty, injustice, famine, floods, natural and man-made disasters, and personal tragedy. Sometimes the only source of optimism in these situations may be recognizing and celebrating the resilience of the survivors.

More often our negativity and psychic burnout comes from our perception of events, not the events themselves. For example, columnist Michael Gantner, points out that some politicians arose fear and gained votes with inflammatory statements about increased crimes. Yet statistically, crime is dropping, while other crucial, but less sensational issues, go unmentioned. There's even good news that gets little fanfare from professional doom sayers: the high school drop out rate has fallen one third since 1960, divorce and abortion rates continue to decline, more people than ever say they are faithful to their spouses, and despite denunciations of our "godless society", church attendance holds steady.

TAKING RISKS

In the midst of change, optimists focus on what they are gaining, while pessimists are clinging to the past and what they perceive they are losing. Wherever there is an opportunity, there is an equal risk.

My wife and I are the proud parents of Alexa Marie Crawford, born on April 24, 1992. We debated a long time about having a child, because we knew that my physical challenge is heredity. Any child we had stood a 50/50 chance of inheriting my handicap. I remember thinking, "How would I feel watching a child struggle? What if he or she is teased like I was?" What selfish thinking! Who am I to say that I am the only person that could handle this physical challenge successfully. It's simply not true. Every year a number of people tell me, "Oh, I could never have handled that", but you never know how strong you really are until you face adversity. Too often we sell ourselves short. We focus on our perceived weaknesses and don't recognize our true strengths.

Donna and I finally realized that anyone who decides to become a parent takes a risk. Just because you're born healthy and able bodied, doesn't mean you're going to live your entire life that way. I was in the delivery room when Alexa was born. Donna had a long, difficult labor. As Alexa was about to be born, my anxiety level was off the chart. Some of the most painful moments of my life came rushing back to me. Then I saw her head emerge and heard her first cry. There is something about the newness of that sound that will be with me forever. Her shoulders came next, then one of her arms with a tiny hand and five normal fingers. She was waving, saying, "Go ahead and count, Daddy." Although I felt I had a special stake in the inventory, I knew that everyone does exactly the same thing, counting fingers and toes the first time they see their child.

Every finger and toe was there; however, Alexa was born with a tiny cleft on her upper lip, almost like a little heart. As I looked at my daughter, she taught me something I had been puzzling about for thirty years. I've often wondered if people thought of me as a handicapped speaker, or a speaker with a handicap. As soon as I looked at my daughter, the cleft was invisible. I thought back to my own parents and how proudly they beamed at the camera when they held me up to be photographed. I've tried to model their level of optimism all my life. My parents showed me their love right away, naming me after my father. And, as Alexa is growing up, my wife and I are going to teach her what my parents taught me—that perfection is a term that applies only to the human shell, not to the human heart or soul. I tell Alexa every day, I'm sure glad I'm her dad.

ROGER CRAWFORD

Roger Crawford is a speaker who has been inspiring, empowering and entertaining audiences throughout the world. Many have even called him the *energizer*, because of his ability to activate and invigorate those who hear him. By building upon optimism as the foundation for personal and professional achievement, he energizes and inspires audiences to embrace their challenges to achieve maximum resilience.

Despite physical limitations, Roger holds certification from the United States Professional Tennis Association as a tennis professional. In high school, he was a four year letterman in tennis with a 47win/6 loss record. At Loyola Marymount University in Los Angeles, he earned a Bachelor of Arts degree in Communications, while becoming the first athlete with a severe disability to compete in a NCAA Division I college sport.

For the past twelve years, Roger has addressed more than 2,000 audiences and over one million people in the

United States and fourteen countries. With his dynamic attitude and irresistible humor, he shares how essential resilience is for success in business and for health and contentment in our lives.

Television audiences across America have enjoyed Roger on Good Morning America, CNBC, Hour of Power and numerous local shows. NBC earned an Emmy Award for their television movie, *In A New Light*, featuring Roger. He is the author of <u>Playing From The Heart</u>, his biography, and <u>Personal Resiliency</u>, an audiocassette album.

PRESENTATIONS

Creating the Champion Within

Emphasis on the topic of <u>resilience</u> as the essential ingredient needed for success in business and for health and contentment in our privates lives.

Playing To Win!

Create renewed motivation by developing strategies for achievement.
Respond positively to negative situations.
Refocusing ourselves to see change as an opportunity.

Take Your Best Shot

Cultivate quality both personally and professionally (The best can always get better.)
Maximize individual and team performance.
Remain upbeat and optimistic in today's competitive world.

OTHER PRODUCTS

Playing From The Heart $17.95
Roger Crawford's Autobiography

Take Your Best Shot! $29.95
Videotape

Personal Resiliency $35.00
4 Cassette Audiotape Album

Playing To Win $150.00
4 Cassette Videotape Album (Designed for youth)

For more information or to
order, please contact:

Crawford & Associates
5658 Oakmont Court
Byron, CA 94514
510-634-8519
Fax 510-634-8517

4

Only The BEST

WHY CUSTOMER SERVICE IS NOT ENOUGH!

By

LISA FORD

SUCCESS

WHY CUSTOMER SERVICE IS NOT ENOUGH!

LISA FORD

What was your latest customer service slogan? "The customer is always right", "The customer comes first." "This is the year of the customer." Have you had a recent customer appreciation week, handed out lapel buttons to all employees stating "Yes, I can" to reflect their empowered attitude? By this time most organizations have involved their employees in a slogan or a customer service seminar. Everyone in management has read the latest books on service (or at least bought the book).

So why is customer service still mediocre at best? Most of the slogans, seminars and books created the right attitude yet no action seemed to follow. Success for individuals as well as organizations comes from action. The best go beyond talking about what they should do or what they are going to do, they simply do it.

In the United States I see three levels of service being

delivered. Those three are rude, indifferent and exceptional. Of these three, which do you mostly receive? Indifference is my vote. Here is one of my recent encounters with indifference. While renting a car, the customer service agent folded the rental contract, told me how to find my car, in which space and then said, "Thank you, sir." Wrong, since I'm a "ma'am". Better yet, why not use "Thank you, Ms. Ford". The misstatement indicated robotic, indifferent service.

Most organizations are great at processing customers, very few excel at serving and satisfying customers. We get processed all the time. Go to the bank and make a deposit, in most cases you get exactly what you need - a correct deposit slip and the amount of money you requested. Did anything occur to leave you with a positive impression of the bank that would keep you loyal? Most likely not. The tellers talked among themselves, did not acknowledge you by name, or thank you. Exceptional service and satisfaction is required to create loyal customers. The process of being served is what's memorable. That personalized transaction is the key to customer retention.

Customer service is not enough, customer satisfaction which leads to retention is the goal.

Here's why - most everyone knows the research and statistics, yet few take the numbers to heart. Research tells us it costs 5-6 times more to attract a new customer than to keep an existing one. Bain & Company reports that if a company retains 5% of their existing customer base, their profits will increase between 25-125%! Have you noticed most companies spend their time, money and energy on attracting new customers and very little is done to keep existing customers. How many times have you seen discount or cash incentives offered by the phone company you use now however, that same offer is not available to you. It's amazing how few organizations have figured out marketing to current customers is good business.

The best strategies for your company to utilize for customer retention are:

1. New glasses for everyone or See your service from your customer's eyes.

There's an old expression "Perception is all there is." The customer's perception is reality and perception is rarely neutral. It is either positive or negative. When being seated in a St. Louis area restaurant, the host pulled out the chair and I can see under the table the floor littered with crumbs and empty cracker packages. When I see the floor I now know what the kitchen looks like and what kind of food to expect - that's the power of perception. Here's the opposite. I take my car to a repair shop that always washes it upon completion. So when I arrive and see my clean car, I'm certain the car's been repaired properly!

The best companies are constantly taking the customer's pulse so they share in the customer perception. Those insights drive their companies to higher levels of service delivery. Some of the methods used to take the customer's pulse include surveys, customer feedback groups and phone calls. All very necessary and useful.

Here are a few creative ones. Weyerhaeuser, in Cottage Grove, Oregon asked their employees to go spend a week as employees of their customers. Shipping managers worked on loading docks at distribution centers, accountants worked as customer service reps at retail centers and as freight drivers. Their goal was to listen and learn to provide insights on how they could improve their work back at Weyerhaeuser. After implementation of the improvements, customers felt Weyerhaeuser's lumber was better than their competitors. In a commodity business that mostly competes on price, what a great achievement!

Be creative with surveys. Grab one of your surveys and fill it out as if you are a customer. Make sure the questions relate to experiences with your company. Is there room for customers to write comments? Boxes and numbers are not enough for them to accurately report their experiences. Make your rating scale different, use the words "love" and "hate". Research does show when customers check the "love" box, you have a loyal retained customer.

Seeing service from your customer's eyes means giving yourself an external view rather than the usual internal one. We all need a new set of glasses on a regular basis. Your challenge: are you asking customers for feedback but not acting on it.

2. Make it memorable or
Redefine customer's expectations.

If you <u>only</u> do what's expected, there is no guarantee that the customer will return. Today's competitive world requires creating memorable experiences that differentiate you from the others. Very few companies have the luxury of offering a product or service that is so unique that customers remain captive.

Here are memorable experiences.

Direct Tire Sales, Watertown Mass., offers customers a free taxi ride or a loaner car to get back home or to work. That one act itself causes customers to call and ask "Is it true you pay for the taxi ride to work?", upon hearing "yes", the actual price of tires is never questioned! If that's not enough, the sparkling clean waiting area has complimentary coffee with "real" cream and fresh croissants along with current magazines.

A dental practice in Maryland hands out flowers to patients on Valentine's Day and lottery tickets to dads on Father's Day. This creative, wacky staff takes any opportunity to put on a costume. Patients schedule appointments around certain holidays, especially Halloween, simply for the experience!

A large paper manufacturer includes a signed packing slip and actual photos of the shipping department employees responsible for the jobs. Their customers love the personal touch.

Your challenge: identify in what six ways have you exceeded and redefined your customer's expectations recently. Now identify the four new things you will do next.

3. Till death do us part or Build partnerships.

Individualize, personalize and customize. The days of the customer being the adversary are long gone. Customers want a partnership that can last a lifetime. As customers we prefer keeping our business in one place if we feel we receive value. We truly are creatures of habit.

Consider these strategies. Sea1st Bank of Seattle realized that the first few months of the relationship are crucial to customer retention. The day of opening a new account the customer is sent a letter of thank you, personalized by the employee who served the new customer. At fourteen days, the employee calls the customer to check on how things are going (did your checks and ATM card arrive?). At 30 days a survey is sent out to solicit feedback on the experience of opening their new account. With these efforts in place, Sea 1st retained five times the number of customers over a three year period.

A florist sends out a card to customers who have used their services to send flowers for a special day. The card reminds them of what was sent last year and how a simple phone call would enable them to do the same this year. With the initial orders, the florist asks if such a card would be desired (obviously to prevent any embarrassing moments).

Your challenge: What are you doing to learn about your customer? Can you use that information to create a partnership? A happy marriage is built on communicating, improving and growing together as you continually learn about your partner. Which of your customers are ready to divorce you or renew the vows?

4. Common sense required or Get back to the basics.

I won't belabor this point. The best organizations usually stand out because they are great at the basics and are slaves to the details. Here's a list of the basics for you to evaluate.

Listening skills.

One of my favorite sayings is "There is a difference between listening and waiting for your turn to talk." Which is your habit?

Phone Skills.

Have you called your own company or department lately? Listen next time and think what your customer experiences. Are there endless recordings, rushed greetings, pleas to "hold please" or numerous transfers? Customers want to talk to only one person. They expect whoever answers the phone to be empowered and able to handle any type of question or problem and do it fast and right the first time!

Recovery skills, dealing with angry customers and handling customer criticism are a few of the other basics where customers expect a professional approach.

You know what the basics are, just make certain you and other staff are doing them daily. No one said this stuff was easy, just that it is common sense.

Your challenge: Create a sense of urgency to be obsessed with the basics and details.

5. Beyond warm bodies or Hire and train the best employees.

Recruiting strategy is a top priority. Starting with the right employees will be the first step in delivering successful service. Too often we've heard managers who are short staffed say, "Hire anybody, get some warm bodies." I'm concerned with that attitude, warm bodies and not much else will be exactly what you get. Now take the warm body comment a step further. If you are a newly hired employee hearing your new manager make that plea, then what are you? Obviously, only a warm body!

Steve Carline, director of sales for a large training firm, says, "We only hire creative, intelligent and articulate people". These words build self-esteem in anyone hearing them.

The best service companies have discovered, hire the attitude. As Herb Kelleher, President of Southwest Airlines says, "People who can fly airplanes are a dime a dozen. Finding people with great attitudes aren't." It is tough to train the attitude and it is certainly easier to train the technical skills. During the interview process, ask questions that uncover how this candidate acts and thinks in customer situations. Here is some of what you can ask, "Give me an example of you providing exceptional customer service." or "What's an example of customer service you've been frustrated by?" Also create customer situations and ask the candidate how they would handle it.

When interviewing someone for a job that requires a lot of phone contact with your customers, do some of the job interview over the phone. Your candidate might be brilliant and charming face to face and lackluster and abrasive on the phone.

Another simple guideline to hiring smart is not to oversell your company. Tell the candidate the good, bad and the ugly of everyday life. Better yet, hire this person for a day or two so they can get a feel for the environment. This gives everyone the chance to determine if "the fit" is right. The last thing you want is "buyer's remorse" from this new employee. Turnover is deadly to customer satisfaction and retention.

Once the person is on board, training is crucial. Too many companies turn an untrained employee loose to serve valuable customers. This is deadly for both the employee and customer. Customers get frustrated when dealing with someone who does not have solutions or the skills to handle tough situations. This usually leads to customer turnover and employee turnover as well. Ryder Truck found that turnover for employees who participated in the company's new training program was 19%. Among the employees who did not participate the rate soared to 41%.

Your investment in training should translate to 2% to 5% of payroll. Motorola invests 3.2% of the payroll into training and sees a 30% gain in productivity for every $1 spent.

Training time must be spent on the technical skills and the soft skills, such as listening and dealing with angry customers. Anyone can teach an employee to "process the customer", but the service and satisfaction skills will differentiate your business.

There is clear and convincing research that excellent customer service employees will result in satisfied retained customers. Here's your challenge: Do you invest as much time in hiring and training new employees as you do in finding and attracting new customers?

6. Act like you mean it or Lead to inspire great service.

Everyone knows this one. As stated previously, most companies only have the attitude and slogans right. Their actions are not aligned accordingly. The best organizations have made customer satisfaction a part of every team and departments goals.

To educate others in their role to serve customers, do job trading. Invite employees from other teams in to observe. Make certain your team goes out to other departments. This exchange can last from one day to a week. Companies successful with this idea make job trading a part of the performance appraisal where employees are responsible for setting up the exchange. If you have some departments in which walls and turfs still exist, job trading succeeds in building a shared understanding of how everyone's work affects the other.

Involve employees in ideas to improve service. One manager asks his team, "If you had my job, what three things would you do to improve customer satisfaction?" This manager is very diligent in following through and implementing the ideas. Employees are an incredible source of ideas when they see evidence of being heard and receive fast feedback on their ideas.

The best organizations even use slogans. The difference is there are aligned policies, procedures, reward systems, recruiting and training to back up their slogans. Words can inspire when employees feel empowered to act accordingly.

Leadership is the most important ingredient in your formula for success. Here's your challenge: When is the last time your leaders listened in on customer calls? Is the leadership arguing loudly and convincingly that quality customer service leads to satisfaction and retention?

Today's customer expects and demands more. They will easily, happily and often quietly take their business elsewhere if service is all they get. Customer service alone is not enough to differentiate you. Your actions must be ones that exceed customer's expectations, build partnerships and create loyalty.

Customer loyalty is earned one transaction at a time. Exceptional service is not magic, it simply requires a daily discipline of execution.

LISA FORD

**Author Of The
#1 Selling Business
Videotape Series
*"How To Give
Exceptional
Customer Service"***

Lisa Ford delivers what her audiences want - practical ideas combined with plenty of opportunities to laugh and relate to her examples. Her content inspires people to increase their personal, team and organization's results.

Lisa is the author of *How To Give Exceptional Customer Service*, the #1 selling business videotape series for the last 3 years in the U.S. She has also authored, *Developing A Customer Retention Program*, co-authored *Building A Customer Driven Organization: The Manager's Role* video and audio tapes, and *Personal Power* audiotapes. She specializes in the field of customer service, customer retention, managing, hiring and training for service excellence. Other popular topics offered by Lisa are on leadership, management, everyday excellence and communications.

Lisa's experience includes working with many of the nation's best: SmithKline Beecham, Equitable, Viacom, CSX and Georgia Power. She presents over 100 speeches and seminars yearly across the United States, United Kingdom and Australia.

Over the years, Lisa has customized numerous videos for clients to use in their ongoing training efforts. She is highly rated and a favorite speaker at the International Customer Service Association where she speaks annually.

Audiences love Lisa's energy, enthusiasm, humor, practical techniques and common sense messages. After her presentations, organizations love the change in attitudes, increased awareness and improved results.

Lisa's Programs Include

- *Why Customer Service Is Not Enough*
  Focus On Satisfaction, Loyalty and Retention
  Exceed Expectations As A Daily Discipline

- *Everyday Excellence*
  Create And Add Value To Increase Your Results
  Maintain An Attitude Of Enthusiasm

- *How To Lead And Manage In Today's Crazy Workplace*
  Understand The Role Of The New Manager
  Love And Master Change

OTHER PRODUCTS

How To Give Exceptional Customer Service $299.95
The Nation's best selling video series. 4 volumes plus workbook covering how to make each contact memorable and keep customers satisfied. Great for training sessions.

How To Give Exceptional Customer Service $79.95
4 audio tape program, great for anyone who has contact with customers. Terrific how-to's, stories and examples.

Developing a Customer Retention Program $59.95
4 audio tapes on how to increase repeat business and build loyalty. Lots of action ideas.

Inspiring Everyday Excellence $10.00
An audio tape recorded live, covering personal excellence, service excellence and leadership excellence. Very motivational.

Six Ways To Be A Service Leader $10.00
An audio tape recorded live, with action steps to exceed customer's expectations and lead to inspire great service. Includes Lisa's memorable dry cleaners story.

Please add $4.00 Shipping & Handling

For more information contact:
Ford Group, Inc.
140 Seville Chase
Atlanta, Georgia 30328
770-394-4860 • FAX 770-394-0034

5

Only The **BEST**

SUCCESS:
IT'S JUST NOT
THAT HARD!

BY

LARRY WINGET

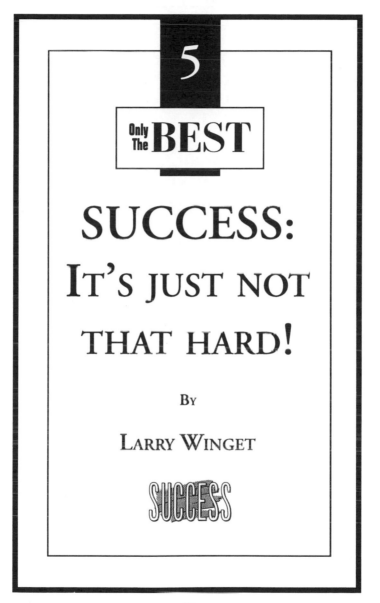

SUCCESS

SUCCESS:
IT'S JUST NOT
THAT HARD!

LARRY WINGET

Not long ago, I was standing on my front porch watching a big thunder cloud approach. My son joined me and asked, "Dad, did you know that cloud is 97% water?" Some how, that fact had eluded me. I guess he learned that in science class and it seemed like an appropriate time to share it. I didn't think too much about it until a few weeks later while I was reading and discovered that a watermelon is 94% water. Did you know that a watermelon missed being a cloud by just 3%? Not much of a difference is it? Just 3%. But even a small difference can have a huge impact on results. This is good news. Because most of us are looking for the hard stuff. Big changes that are hard to learn and even harder to implement in order to make big changes in our lives.

As a professional speaker, I am in front of several thousand people each year. These are people from all walks of life, representing many different industries, and from all parts of the world. They are blue collar, white collar and no collar. And while each person and each audience is unique in many ways, they all still have some things in common: they want to know how they can be more successful, more prosperous, and happier. I have found that while we are all different, we all are still alike in at least these three areas. And it doesn't matter what our definition of success is, how much money we have or don't have, or how happy we are or aren't, we want more! Don't you? Don't you want to know how to be more successful, be more prosperous and be happier? Of course you do. Well, good news - it's just not that hard. In fact, it is remarkably simple. Success, prosperity, and happiness are all based on a few simple principles. Here are just a few:

Know the flow. There is a flow to all success. When you discover the flow and move into the flow you are bound to be more successful. In fact, there is no way to avoid success at that point. This is the flow: everything gets better for us when we get better. Business gets better for us when we get better for it. Sales improve when we improve. Relationships get better when we get better. Understanding this flow of success will improve your results in every area of your personal and professional life. Just know that everything in your life will get better when you get better and nothing in your life will get better until you get better.

Decide. If you want to do something, then just decide to do it. If you want to be something, then decide to be it. If you want to have something, then make a decision to have it.

You are what you are, do what you do, and have what you have all because you decided it on some level. If you had decided something different, then your experience would have been different. So make a decision at the highest level to be, do and have to best of everything in your life.

Believe. If you want to be more, do more, and have more, then believe that it is possible. Your beliefs will always manifest themselves first in your actions and then in your results. The stronger your belief, the faster the results.

Forget blame. Your results are your responsibility. You are where you are in life because of the actions you have taken. Your results are not the fault of the government, the economy, your boss, your in-laws, your spouse, or the weather. We spend so much time looking for excuses outside of ourselves. We even have a list of reasons on the tip of our tongue for not being more and having more. In my opinion, a reason is just an excuse that has been rationalized to make it sound better. But bottom line: blaming anything outside of ourselves is a waste of effort and never moves us closer to where we want to be. When you want to know why you don't have more, just go to the mirror.

Forget guilt. Guilt serves no purpose. You can't go back and change one thing that has ever happened. We spend so much time saying "if only I hadn't." Well . . . you did! Big deal. Forgive yourself and move on.

Forget luck. People get what they get because they are ready for it, not because the world favors them over someone else. Increase your deservability and take some chances and more good stuff will come your way. Know that you can have anything you want when you feel that you are deserving of it and when you take the proper steps to make it happen.

Make your own circumstances. If things are not as you wish them to be, then change them. You are in complete control. Take charge of your life and make things happen the way you want them to.

Focus on the present. What you are doing right now is the most important thing in your life. What you are doing now will determine what you have in the future. It's not what you have done or will do that matters. So examine your life and make sure that you are doing things at each moment that move you closer to where you want to be. Only by doing that will you produce the kind of life you want to have.

Look for the good in everything. Even if what you are going through seems bad at the moment, there is a lesson to be learned. And any time we learn anything, it's positive. Growth, change, and new lessons are always good for us.

Be flexible. Flexibility is one of the true keys to success in relationships with customers, co-workers, family, and friends. It will also help you deal more effectively with the challenges you will face in our ever-changing society and business environment. And while I am on the subject, remember that change is about process (how we do things) and not about purpose (why we do things). Our purpose must always be about serving others. Become more flexible with process and less flexible with purpose.

Serve others. Your rewards are in direct proportion to your service. The more you serve others through your words, your products, and your life, the more you will be served. The world is reciprocal. There is a Universal Law that governs everything. It is the Law of Cause and Effect. For every action there is a reaction. The action you must take to get a positive reaction is the action of service to other people. When you make serving others your primary goal there is nothing that can stand in the way of you getting more from life at every level.

Love. What? That's right. Love in these areas:

Love what you do or do something else. You can't be really good at anything that you don't love doing. People will do more business with you, and enjoy your company more when they know and can tell that you love what you do. Love brings about passion and passion is always marketable. I have discovered that most people just don't pay much attention to what you say. In fact, most people won't even believe what you say. However, they will pay attention to see if *you* believe what you say. And your belief and passion will show when you love what you are doing.

Love the people you are doing it for. Your family, your customers, your co-workers, etc. Love them even when they aren't very lovable. Loving them just means that you want the best for them and that you are willing to give them your best . . . regardless.

Love yourself. If you don't hold yourself in high esteem, it will be impossible to hold others in high esteem. You are valuable. You are unique. Discover your uniqueness and learn to exploit it in the service of others and you are guaranteed success, happiness, and prosperity.

Give. Give away some of everything you have. Never pass up an opportunity to give. A wise man once said, "A rejected opportunity to give is a lost opportunity to receive." Success, happiness and prosperity are life principles based on flow. Start the flow and keep it coming into your life by giving to those who need it.

> **Give advice sparingly.**
> **Give love unconditionally.**
> **Give stuff freely.**
> **Give time carefully.**
> **Give yourself wholeheartedly.**

Lighten up. Don't take things so seriously. Just ask yourself: Will it matter ten years from now? Or even ten minutes from now? Life is to be enjoyed, not worried over and fretted about. Read humor books and listen to humor tapes. Call me, I will sell you mine. Buy a whoopee cushion and some red socks. Ask little kids how to have fun . . . they know!

Study success. There is more good stuff out there on how to be successful in every area of your life than ever before in history. You can get it in a book like this one, or on an audio tape, CD ROM, video, on the Internet, or your television, your radio and who knows where else. We do not fail due to lack of information on how to succeed. We fail because we do not find, study, and implement the information.

You are responsible TO others but not FOR others. This is a biggy. Do right. Honor and serve others in all that you say and do. Then be done with it. If they disapprove, or criticize, or don't like you or what you have said or done, that is their problem; not yours. You are only responsible for giving others your very best, not for their response or reaction to it.

Do something. Action makes things happen. So get started. But where do I start? It doesn't really matter. Just get the motion going. If you start and find out you are doing the wrong thing, you will know quicker. Remember, you don't have to be good to start, but you do have to start to be good.

> **You don't have to be good to start,**
> **but you do have to start to be good.**

We could all do more than we are currently doing. No matter how busy you are now, you could do more, couldn't you? Sure you could. The good news is that even a small increase in action can have a dramatic impact on our results.

> **After all is said and done,**
> **more is said than done.**

Do the easy stuff: recycle - don't litter - don't talk in movie theaters - don't smack your gum - listen more - talk less - read more - think more - walk more - don't interrupt - give up judgment in all forms - don't whine or gripe - don't eat or drink too much - don't smoke - send birthday cards - use good grammar - be on time - say thank you more often - spend more money on fewer things - avoid speaking in absolutes - don't cuss - enjoy the differences in people - be *for* stuff instead of against stuff - honor every one - laugh a lot!

Expect the best. What you expect is what you usually get. When you learn to expect the best, your chances of getting it go way up!

Be prepared for the worst. Read the books, listen to the tapes, go to the seminars, and talk to the experts, so when the worst happens (and it will) you will be ready for it.

Celebrate it all. Life is too short to be miserable, even for one instant! So look for ways to celebrate everything that happens. Can you celebrate the bad stuff too? Of course, because remember: no matter how bad it is, it could always be worse. Never say something stupid like "it couldn't possibly get worse." If there is one thing I'm sure of, it's that it could be worse!

> **Expect the best.**
> **Be prepared for the worst.**
> **Celebrate it all!**

Is that all there is to it? Of course not. This is not

the end-all, do-all, and be-all list to be more successful, more prosperous, and happier. I never intended for it to be. There is a lot more than this. However, this is most of what you need in order to have much better results than you are currently experiencing. If you never did anything other than these things, you would definitely achieve more than you have been in the past. So don't make it so hard.

> **Success does not come from doing the hard stuff, it comes from doing the simple stuff really well.**

LARRY WINGET

Larry Winget began life on a chicken ranch in Muskogee, Oklahoma. He has driven a bookmobile and was one of the first male telephone operators in the Bell System. He has shoveled manure, swept floors, sold, managed, and been the company president. He has experienced both incredible business success and total business failure. However, he is proof that you can go belly-up in business without going face down in failure.

Larry is currently an internationally recognized speaker and seminar leader. He is the author of more than a dozen books and the creator of many audio/video learning systems, as well as lots of other unique personal development products.

Larry is an active member of the National Speakers Association and a charter member of the Oklahoma Speakers Association. He speaks on the subjects of Success,

Leadership, Teambuilding, Being Customer Obsessed, and Prosperity. He is also widely known as a humorist and all 'round funny guy. Regardless of the topic, you can be assured that his material is centered around universal principles that will work for anyone, at any time, and in any business. Plus, Larry reads over one hundred books per year to make sure that his stuff is current and that he knows what he's talking about.

Larry believes that success in either our personal or professional life is not hard. It simply comes down to knowing what to do and doing it. He is committed to helping everyone understand that they deserve the best and can have it, when they follow a few simple principles. Known for his unique style, Larry's down-to-earth, humorous, bottom-line approach makes his "stuff" fresh, fun, and easy to implement.

Larry Winget has discovered his uniqueness and learned to exploit it in the service of others. His symbol is the exclamation point. His heroes are Tarzan, Superman, and The Lone Ranger. His dogs are Elvis and Nixon. His wife is Rose Mary. His boys, Tyler and Patrick. His philosophy is, "Expect the best. Be prepared for the worst. Celebrate it all!"

▆ OTHER PRODUCTS ▆

The Ya Gotta's For Success! — Larry's most popular book $12.95
Over 200 pages covering 30 principles of success that will help you discover the things "ya gotta" do and be in order to have the success you deserve.

The Ya Gotta's For Success! Audio Cassette $9.95
Larry's most popular keynote address. Includes his stories of Tarzan, Superman, The Lone Ranger, Sonic, Radio Shack and more! Motivational, inspirational and humorous!

Money Stuff — Book $11.95
How to increase prosperity, attract riches, experience abundance and have more money. This book ties the spiritual principles of love, service, and giving straight to the bottom line.

Stuff That Works Every Single Day — Book $9.95
365 daily readings that address various principles of personal and professional development.

The Little Red Book Of Stuff That Works Book $7.95
647 one-liners of advice, instructions, ideas, thoughts, observations, truths, notions, hints, philosophies, theories, witticisms, opinions, quotations, and other great stuff that works.

Just Do This Stuff — Book $7.95
How to really DO success. Thirty five topics with step-by-step action lists to follow on each topic. This is the practical application of success. No lofty philosophy, just practical stuff to do that brings results!

Larry's Stuff Package • *All six items above.* $50.00

Positees™ *by UNGAWA GEAR*™ *(Hanes Beefy-T shirts in XL only)* $20.00
• *UNGAWA! Neon green on white shirt*
• *Shut up, stop whining, and get a life! Neon colors on gray shirt*
• *Think positive or don't think at all! Purple & black on gray shirt*
• *Larry - The World Tour Black and red on gray shirt*

Please include $5.00 shipping and handling • *Mastercard and Visa Welcome*
For a complete catalog of Larry's books, audio and video learning systems, and other unique personal development products as well as information on Larry's keynote presentations and seminars, please contact:

Win Seminars!
P. O. Box 700485
Tulsa, Oklahoma 74170
918 745-6606 • 800 749-4597
Fax 918 747-3185

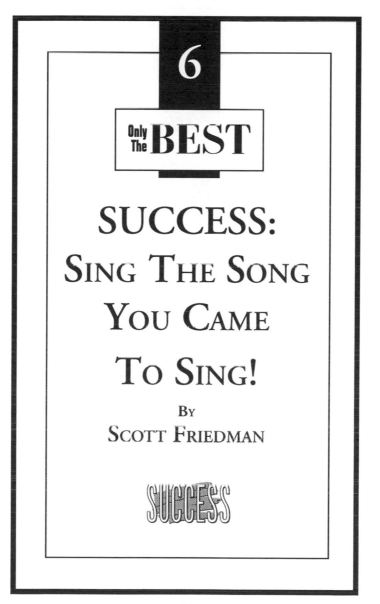

6

Only The BEST

SUCCESS:
SING THE SONG
YOU CAME
TO SING!

BY
SCOTT FRIEDMAN

SUCCESS

SUCCESS: SING THE SONG YOU CAME TO SING!

SCOTT FRIEDMAN

Success! It means different things to different people. Have you ever sat down and asked yourself, what does *success* mean to you? What would it take for you to consider yourself a success? We all say we want success, but what does that really mean?

Success Step 1: Define Success

The first step on the path to success is to clarify your own unique definition of success. Many people in our society define success in financial terms. Malcolm Forbes coined the phrase, "The one who dies with the most toys wins!" reflecting the popular value that the acquisition of material possessions is what the game of life is all about. I'd like to offer my version of this saying: The one who dies with the most toys, still dies.

I think the important questions to ask yourself in defining success are: What endures? What brings you joy? What brings joy to those you love? Who and what do you care about? In what do you take pride? When it's all said and done, what will make you feel your life has been worthwhile?

In my experience, relationships are more rewarding and far more enduring than material possessions. I believe that the quality of life is determined primarily by the quality of our relationships. *To love and be loved* — that's "where it's at" for me! Only you can determine "where it's at" for you.

In order to get in touch with what really matters to you, what constitutes success to you, it is helpful to take yourself far enough away from the pressures and distractions of your world so *you can hear the song* your heart wants to sing. Some of us have buried it so deeply or ignored it for so long that we have to get very, very quiet and listen very hard to hear its gentle strains. *What song did you come to sing?* Once you've determined what your life song is, then it's up to you to make sure it gets sung. *Are you hitting some of the brightest, clearest, finest notes of your life's song?*

I'd like to share a few chords of my life's song with you! If I'm spending quality time with family and friends, if I'm healthy, if I'm challenging myself to keep growing professionally, personally and spiritually, if I'm being true to myself, and making a difference in the lives of those around me, then by my definition — *the only one that really matters* — I am a success!

By knowing what is important to me, I can set up my life to be successful. You can do the same thing! So put down this book and think for a few minutes about what is important to you. Just start writing whatever comes to mind. After you've put all of your thoughts on paper, go back and pull out the most important ones to create your personal definition of success — without which you're not likely to achieve it! So pick up that pen and paper and start writing your own definition of success! Don't worry; it's not etched in stone! You're allowed to modify or change it — in fact, that's required, as you evolve and mature and learn more about life and yourself. But it's still necessary to keep a "tune" in your head if you intend to sing!

How you define success:
Success to me,_____,
is _____

_____

_____

_____

_____

_____

_____

Success Step 2: Manage Your Thoughts

Once you've defined success for yourself, you are on your way! Now, it's time for the next step on your path to success. In fact, this step is far more than one step! It is so important that most of the truly successful people I've observed place it as a companion step to every other step along the path! For the single most important step — the one that distinguishes the winners from the losers in the quest for success — is how well they manage their thoughts. The real winners know that *SUCCESS IS AN INSIDE JOB!*

How well do you manage your thoughts? To become a success, to sing your life's song, requires that you manage your thoughts to achieve that end. If you have great command over what you think, then you really are on your way to success! But think about this: Most people think about *what they do* and *how they feel,* but seldom think about *what they think about!* Yet it's what you think about that determines what you do and how you feel. So ask yourself, *What do you think about?* It's something to think about!

Choose Positive Thoughts

Each of us has our own unique perspective on the world. It's our reality. Without even thinking, we're thinking. We can't stop thinking, but we can change our thoughts. We can influence and even choose our thoughts.

The process of choosing your thoughts starts with knowing your desired outcomes in any given situation. As you catch yourself thinking about other things — especially things like past unproductive relationships, "If only's," and mistakes you've made — immediately replace those thoughts with thoughts of the outcomes you want, because what you think about is what you get! Think you can have what you want, you can. Think you're not good enough, you're not. Think the world is out to get you, it is. Thoughts really do create results — the ones we desire or the ones we don't — depending on what we dwell on!

Trade in Blame and Pity for Responsibility

It's so common that it's considered "human nature" to conjure excuses or look for someone else to blame when life doesn't work out. The truth is that if we kicked the person responsible for our lives' not working out the way we want, we wouldn't be able to sit down for a week!

One thing is for certain: If we don't take responsibility for creating our lives, we allow other people and circumstances to shape our lives by default. Then we reactivily sing a song we didn't come to sing. Those who do take responsibility for their lives seem to have a great deal more ability to shape their lives! *What song did you come to sing? Start singing, and don't go the grave with music still in you.*

The other side of the *blame* coin is *pity*! You've thrown

the party, the self-pity party, where just *you* gather round, to celebrate all the things you don't like about you . . . and your life!

By choosing our thoughts, we can shake the blame and pity syndrome, and set ourselves up to be happy. Ralph Waldo Emerson said that thoughts rule the world. We cannot control everything that happens in our lives, but the way that we evaluate our experiences shapes the way we think in the future. Pay close attention to the way you evaluate situations. As things happen, *listen* to what you are thinking and saying to yourself. Then consciously focus on using each experience as an opportunity to create thoughts that serve you better.

Model Good Thought Managers

Art Linkletter said, "Things happen the best for the people who make the best out of the things that happen." This is a form of thought management that is perhaps best developed by modeling someone who has mastered it. My Grandmother has a special way of turning all of her experiences into learning lessons.

Grandma Fred, short for Fredella, at 82, is the best *thought manager* I know. That's the reason she's so hip and stays so young. She dresses young; she acts young; she thinks young! She's beat cancer and a stroke, lost my Grandfather, an apartment to an earthquake, and has had a few other assorted dramas along the way. And the amazing thing is that she's as happy as can be! She's out there playing tennis, dancing, and exploring 'till way past the clock strikes twelve.

If there's a way to make it work, she'll find it. Seven years ago, about a year after my Grandfather had passed away, Grandma Fred invited Lance, a handsome, rough-looking, well-built 25-year-old Italian boy to move in with her. Lance had worked in security in the building, and had become good friends with my Grandparents. He left that job to become a male dancer at a local night club — not a profession any of my high school or college buddies had chosen to pursue. Lance needed to cut his overhead and needed a mother figure in his life. Grandma needed some help around the apartment and a little companion-ship — so she said! Could she possibly have been a Grandma on the prowl? Nahhh! She was just making life work. She was managing her thoughts. She was a suc-cess! Lance now lives in Dallas and has joined the World Wrestling Federation. No, she didn't go with him.

In January of 1994, Grandma was a little too close to the center of that California Earthquake. Hey, it wasn't her fault! As Grandma describes it, it was as if someone just picked up this huge apartment complex and started shaking it. Everything in her apartment was shattered, glass was everywhere, and her apartment was condemned. To this day, it still hasn't been repaired. What a quick way to lose your clothes, your possessions, and your privacy!

In her good-natured way, she said, "This too will pass." And, typically, she managed to find humor in the situation. She joked that after the quake she sent away for an earthquake survival guide and got back a map to Kansas! No matter the drama, she's one good stage director! She's a woman in control of her thoughts. She inspired this poem:

Grandma Fred's Poem

You can be just thirty-three and over the hill,
Or eighty-three going on twenty-nine!
The young-at-heart don't care about birthdays or years;
They know age is a state of mind!

You're never too old to be young,
So make love and laughter part of the plan;
The best thing in life is to die young
As old as you possibly can!

Program Yourself for Success

By now it should be fairly obvious that a positive attitude is the key to successful thought management — and to success! Many people take the problems of each day to bed with them, and wake up thinking about those same problems. Add to that the negative impact of watching the evening news just before bedtime, and it's not a surprise people have trouble getting out of bed in the morning!

So how, you may ask — if you aren't naturally quite as positive as Grandma Fred — can you *learn to manage your thoughts* better? You can actually program yourself for success simply by asking yourself a series of questions when you awake in the morning. Determine the questions that have the greatest impact for you, and then start every morning with them. Here are a few questions that work for me. Try them on for effect.

Question #1 - What do I have to be grateful for? The fact that there is not a chalk outline around your body when you wake up is something to be grateful for. Count your blessings every morning. If you look at some of the unfortunate situations that could be bestowed upon you, from a terrible disease to a natural disaster, your worries pale by comparison. When you're focusing on what works in your life, then you're not thinking about what doesn't work.

Question #2 - How can I make a difference in someone's life today? The quickest way to make your thoughts more cheerful is to cheer up somebody else. Focus on what you can do for someone else, and you'll be amazed at the side benefits. *Fragrance always clings to the hand that gives roses.*

Question #3 - What great thing is going to happen to me today? If we expect great things to   happen,   great things have a way of sneaking into our lives. I live by the assumption that every inconvenience I encounter is just an opportunity for something good to happen; that conflicts are just blessings in disguise. As I am writing this in Chicago's O'Hare airport, my flight is delayed for three hours. I begin looking for the blessing. Suddenly, there it is! A friend I haven't seen in five years shows up out of nowhere! His plane is delayed too. We spend a wonderful hour catching up. A true blessing. And then there is the additional blessing that I have an unexpected block of uninterrupted time to write this chapter! Look for the blessings and they will appear.

Because the first fifteen minutes of the morning will set the tone for the rest of your day, it's also a good idea to start your morning with a happiness pledge. It's silly, but it's almost guaranteed to kick-start your day!

THE HAPPINESS PLEDGE:
I, _____, promise to think about what I think about, and to give myself permission to be happy — because I'm good enough, I'm smart enough, and dog-gone it, I don't care if people like me! I like me! I am awesome! YESSS!!! [Accompanying gesture: Make fist with right hand and pull right elbow quickly in to side.]

By starting each day with some sort of "happy ritual" we improve our odds of having a great day. We are responsible for our own happiness! As Abraham Lincoln said, "People are about as happy as they decide to be."

Reframe Challenges into Opportunities

The biggest test of how we manage our thoughts comes when life deals us a situation we don't like. Every situation allows us the opportunity to get bitter or to get better, to get discouraged or to get determined. But every experience in our lives brings with it some sort of gift: gifts to learn, to grow, to think in terms of new possibilities. The failures in our lives should not dis-empower us, because they are just part of the process. Struggle, challenge and pain can be transformational power if we are open to the lessons. They are gifts that serve as a wake up call, a gut check, a sign to take a look inside and get creative about what we want. Unfortunately, all too often we view mistakes and failures as a destination rather than just another part of the journey.

When challenges start to get the best of you, it's time to reframe your thoughts. Suppose, for instance, there were no such thing as success or failure, a right or wrong way of doing things, but only lessons to be learned that generate wisdom leading to better choices. Would you approach life differently? In singing your life's song, you're going to hit a few false notes, but that's usually when we hear the best wisdom, if we're listening!

Success Step 3: Sing Your Song

When life isn't working quite as you'd planned
And something seems to be wrong,

It's either time to adjust the tune
Or completely change the whole song.

Life's joys and regrets, when it's all said and done,
Come not from life's games lost or won,
But from whether you sang what you came here to sing,
Or left with your life's song unsung!

Success! It means different things to different people. First define it, then make sure your thoughts are congruent with the song you came to sing, and then SING YOUR SONG! Success is an <u>automatic by-product</u>! Life is a musical composed of two songs: the one you wanted to sing, and the song that you actually do sing. The moment of truth — the most humble hour in our lives — is when we compare those two songs.

To make sure that your life is a reflection
of the *life song* you came to sing,
Watch your thoughts,
for your thoughts become your words.
Watch your words,
for your words become your actions.
Watch your actions,
for your actions become your habits.
Watch your habits
for your habits become your destiny.

SCOTT FRIEDMAN, CSP*

Scott Friedman is a humorous speaker with a valuable message. Scott teaches audiences to open their minds through laughter, while sharing "how to" techniques and practical ideas. He illustrates an approach to becoming a victor of change instead of a victim.

Scott is two time Past-President of the Colorado Chapter of the National Speakers Association and has earned the CSP (Certified Speaking Professional), designation, by the National Speakers Association.

After graduating from Southern Methodist University, in Dallas, in 1978 with a degree in Marketing and a minor in Psychology, Scott worked as Marketing Director for Duff's Smorgasboard, a National food chain. After developing many successful promotional programs to increase sales he moved onto other sales and marketing opportunities. For the next two-and-a-half years Scott became one of the top salespeople for AB Hirschfeld Press, the largest Printing company west of the Mississippi. He then entered Public Speaking as Marketing Director of SpeechMasters, a company that trains lawyers, public speakers and executives in effective presentation skills. Scott doubled their business by carving out new market niches while receiving acclaimed speech training. Scott became a full-time professional speaker in 1986, and has been sharing practical ideas and 'how to' techniques on sales motivation, humor, and creating results.

Scott has discovered a way to instantly connect with almost any audience, regardless of age, creed, or gender. "Humor creates an immediate bond," says Scott. With the precision of a surgeon, Scott uses humor to remove negative, non-productive feelings and install a positive, fresh approach towards work, relationships, and life!

*CSP - Certified Speaking Professional

OTHER PRODUCTS

Audio Tape - The Best Way to Predict the Future is to Create It $10
An innovative approach to creating the future, this renown program teaches techniques in creating results, mastering change, boosting self-esteem, exploring the positive uses of humor, and building better relationships. Treat yourself to a grand shot in the arm as you walk away with needed answers about creating your future.

Using Humor For a Change $9.50
With change, uncertainty, and job insecurity sweeping through America today, stress is at record highs. If you can laugh at your stress, you can survive it. Explore 101 creative ideas to lighten up the work place.

Please add $3.00 Shipping & Handling

For more information contact:
Scott Friedman, CSP
1563 S. Trenton Ct.
Denver, CO 80231
303-671-7222 • FAX 303-368-5781

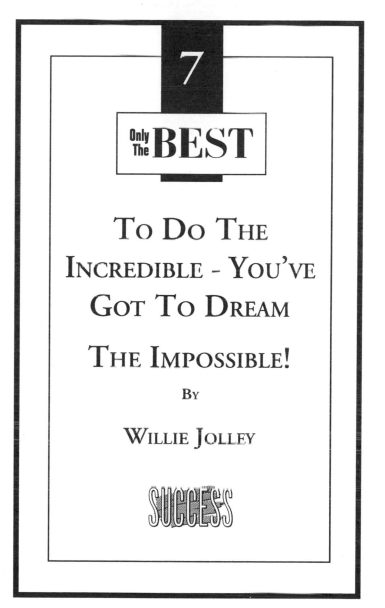

7

Only The **BEST**

To Do The Incredible - You've Got To Dream The Impossible!

By

Willie Jolley

SUCCESS

To Do The Incredible - You've Got To Dream The Impossible!

Willie Jolley

"It must be borne in mind that the tragedy of life does not lie in not reaching your goals, the tragedy lies in not having a goal to reach for! It is not a calamity to die with your dreams unfulfilled but it is a calamity not to dream. It is not a disaster to be unable to capture your ideals but it is a disaster to have no ideals to capture. It is not a disgrace not to reach the stars but it is a disgrace to have no stars to reach for! Not failure but low aim is sin!" Dr. Benjamin Mays

My co-workers told me I had to be crazy, as they stood at the door and watched me walk those 100 long steps to my old broken down car. They laughed because they knew that the car was about to die and all I had to my name was $200.00. They said, "You must be insane! You're going to leave your good government job because you've got a dream?

You want to do what?! You want to be a speaker? You want to start your own company? You want to write books? You want to do radio and television? You want to Be Great? *Stop Dreaming*! Get Real! You don't even have enough money to fix your car!" I could hear them laughing louder and louder with every step I took. The further I walked, the louder they laughed and laughed and laughed! The last thing I heard them say was "He'll be back. He'll be back. Ha! Ha! Ha! He'll be back!"

Well, they were right! I did go back! But this time I returned as a consultant, driving a Mercedes Benz ...making about eight times as much as when I left! In just a few short years I had become the president of my own company. I had a staff and a beautiful office. I had spoken to over one million people. I had written books and recorded albums and motivational books on tapes. I had a syndicated radio show and had just been elected president of the National Capitol Speakers Association. And I was having a ball!

Did the Mercedes, the staff, or the money make me a success? NO! Those were just the by-products of my learning the recipe for success. What was it? What was the key? What was the main ingredient? What was the thing that kept me from turning around and listening to my co-workers? What kept me from believing my co-workers and made me step out all by myself? What was the thing that was essential to my success? *What was it?* It was ... THE POWER OF A DREAM!

Dreams are the seed for success - the main ingredient for success. Michael Jordan was asked in an interview, "What makes you such an outstanding basketball player?" His answer was that he was cut from his ninth grade basketball team because he was not good enough! He went home that night and dreamed about doing impossible things with a basketball, so he could prove that the coach had made a mistake. Once he could dream it and visualize it on the inside (in his head), then he knew that he could create it on the court ... *on the outside*! Duke Ellington was asked what was the key to his musical masterpieces. "I dream a lot," he said. Walt Disney was asked how he created Disneyland after having two nervous breakdowns and going bankrupt. His answer was, "I just kept on dreaming!" And the list goes on and on and on. You've got to have a DREAM!

If you took a corn seed, dug a hole, planted the seed, covered it over and watered it ... it would grow into a corn stalk. And from that corn seed would come an endless amount of other corn seeds. If you took an acorn and planted it, covered it over and watered it everyday ... it would grow into an oak tree. The same is true for your dreams. If you can take a dream, create it in your mind, plant in your heart and water it, it too will grow! Cavett Robert said it so aptly: "Anything your mind can conceive and your heart can believe, you can achieve." But you must know how to water it. You water it by saying, "I believe I can do it! I believe I can do it! In fact, I know I can do it!"

It sounds elementary, it sounds simple, but that does not mean that it is easy. It is not easy. It is difficult because we first have to overcome the negative seeds that have been planted in our minds over the span of our lifetimes. In discussing success, Les Brown shared with me that the hardest part of his success was not making a million dollars! The hardest part was just believing that it was possible that he could make a million dollars!

The Bible says that without a vision a people perish and that all things are possible to those who believe. I have found it to be true that it is absolutely necessary to have a vision of the future and where you fit, or you tend to become a "mis-fit" and drift with the wind. With no vision, a person can perish. With a vision, that person can flourish! You've got to have a dream. And the bigger the dream, the bigger the rewards.

Mike Murdock shares with his audiences that there are two types of dreams, mosquito dreams and elephant dreams. If you take two mosquitoes (a male and a female) and they decide to start a family, they can have a new teeny weenie baby mosquito within twenty-four hours! If you take a male and a female elephant and they decide to start a family, they must wait for twenty-three months! But the results are massive! I believe if you're going to dream, you might as well dream BIG dreams! It might take a little longer, but, is it well worth the wait!

Once you get a dream - and it's a big dream, is that all it takes to be a success? No! It is just the starting point, the seed for success. Success is like cooking soup. You must start with the base, but then you must add other ingredients in order to develop an outstanding product. After you get a dream then you must add a "do"! You must ACT on your dreams. You must take action and go after your dreams. If not, then you have a wish, and wishes have no substance. Wishes make the soup bland and watery. We all have wished upon a star or thrown pennies into the wishing well and never really expected those wishes to come true. They are just fantasies. A dream that has no action will never become more than a wish.

So what else is needed to make this success soup a reality? The next ingredient to add to the mix is *desire*! Desire - you must want it bad! I remember speaking at a school where I met a young man who had the physique of Atlas. Six-foot-five and 250 pounds of pure muscle. He came up after my presentation. I shook his hand and asked him what he wanted to do when he "grew up". "Play pro football," was his response. Yes, he had the body and the physical attributes but I wondered if he had the heart. "Do you want to be great and do you want it bad?" I asked. He said yes. I asked if he wanted it real bad, and he said yes. Then I asked the definitive question. Did he want it bad enough to run through a brick wall, if necessary. He looked away and shyly said, "Nah, I don't want it that bad." As I looked up at him, I explained that until he developed the desire to want it badly enough to go through a brick wall, success in football would be difficult to achieve because mere talent and ability are still not enough. Millions of people are not using their talents but are working jobs they settled for because the competition was too tough! They didn't have that little bit of extra "umph" to rise above the masses. They didn't have that little bit of extra which makes such a big difference. There was no desire. They didn't want it badly enough!

You must dream it! Make a conscious determined decision to *do it!* Then take action! Desire is the element that separates the men from the boys, the women from the girls and the achievers from the mere dreamers. Desire is the element that some call, "the little extra that makes the big difference." You've got to want to be a success and you've got to want to be excellent. You've got to want to make your dreams into realities and you've got to want to achieve greatness. You've got to want it ... and want it *bad!*

The great ones want it bad. Larry Bird is an example. After he had won the NBA title and the MVP award, he still went to the gym everyday and spent hours shooting practice shots. Walter Payton, after he had won the rushing title, still ran up a mountain everyday with weights on his back and legs! To be great it is absolutely necessary that you want it bad. You must stoke the fire of desire. You've got to want it so badly that you are willing to go through the brick wall. You may never have to go through that brick wall but you must be willing. To be a success at any level, you must want that more than anything else! The great football coach, Vince Lombardi said, "The difference between a successful person and others is not a lack of strength, not a lack of knowledge, but rather in a lack of will." DESIRE!

Do you want it badly? Are you *really* serious about your success? Are you willing to go the extra mile? Are you willing to do the little extras that make a big difference? Are you willing to stay up late and get up early? Are you willing to experience pain and rejection as you pursue your dream? Are you willing to do that which is uncomfortable, to fight for your dream? Are you serious? Are you serious about what you're doing or are you just dabbling?

Ask yourself the questions. What would I do if I were serious?. What goals would I pursue? What would I continue doing and what would I discontinue doing? What non-productive, time wasting activities would I eliminate? What would I do if I were really serious? When you ask yourself the right questions, your mind will give you the right answers. Once you get the answers, take a sheet of paper and write them down. Read them and start to work on the list. Realize that no matter what you are presently doing, you can do more. You can accomplish and achieve more, *if* you are willing to get serious.

When I left my job, I did an exercise that I want to share with you. While sitting in a small hotel room in Nashville Tennessee, I took out a piece of paper and completed this exercise. Imagine going to the doctor and he says that he has good and bad news. The bad news is that you only have one year to live, that's it! The good news is that this illness is a rare, one-of-a-kind illness that allows you a very distinct luxury. Anything you attempt, you will achieve. It is impossible for you to fail! What ten things would you go after if you knew you could not fail and would definitely achieve them. List more if you can. That list is your dream list — all the things that your heart has hidden away because your mind is afraid to attempt them.

Take that list and read it daily until you actually start to believe it; until you really start to believe that you can achieve the incredible; until you grasp the fact that all things really are possible if you can just believe! Believe in yourself and your dreams. Have clear and concrete knowledge of your purpose - your reason for being here. Have faith that God would not give you a dream that you could not achieve. Dr. Robert Schuller says that dreams do not come out of the blue, but rather out of the mind of God, and He matches the dream with the dreamer! Yet, it is up to us to do the work to make those dreams into realities.

My son and I were riding by the building where I used to work, where my co-workers stood at the door and laughed at me. My son who was about eight years old at the time asked, "Daddy, isn't that where you used to work?" I said "Yes.' He said, "Daddy, did you get fired?" I answered, "No, I quit"! When I said that I could see the pain etched on his face because he has heard me say millions of times, "Never give up, never give up, no matter what , never give up!" I stopped the car and looked him in the eye and told him, "William, I quit!...not because I was giving up, but because I was *going* up!"

Friends, sometimes you have to quit things that keep you down, keep you bound, and make you frown. You have to realize that to do the incredible, you must first dream the impossible. Dream! Then take positive, determined action. Pursue excellence in all that you do. Develop great desire and commitment to reach your dreams. Then take full responsibility for your success. Get serious, and in short order you will see your dreams sprout, grow and blossom! Dream The Impossible! Go Forth and Be Bold!

WILLIE JOLLEY

Amazing...Intense... Exciting... Innovative... Versatile... and Dynamic are terms commonly used to describe the unique talents of **Willie Jolley.** He is a multi-talented speaker, singer, author and media personality who is literally burning up the speaking and motivation industry. Many consider him to be *"...the fastest growing motivational force in America today!"* Zig Ziglar says, *"Willie Jolley is a tremendous talent who brings power and excitement to every audience"*, **Brian Tracy** says *"Willie Jolley is perhaps the most extraordinary speaking/singing talent emerging in America today."* After hearing him speak, **Les Brown and Gladys Knight** were so taken by his talents that they immediately invited him to be part of their **National Music and Motivation Dream Team Tour.**

Willie Jolley has created a new kind of motivation called **"Inspir-Tainment"** which mixes speaking and singing with inspiration, entertainment, education and motivation... and it hits with *the force of a hurricane.* **A Dynamic Speaker, a Powerful Singer, an Engaging Author plus an Exciting Entertainer...ALL IN ONE PERSON!**

Born in Washington DC , **Willie Jolley** got his entrepreneurial start as a newspaper boy who creatively designed a distribution system employing his friends and building one of the area's most profitable routes. **Willie** went on to start a singing group which became a local success story and signed his first record deal at the age of 17. The group broke up, but he continued to perform and helped pay his way through college and graduate school, where he received a B.A. in Psychology and Sociology from American University and a Masters Degree from Wesley Theological Seminary, by singing jingles and performing in local night clubs. He soon became Washington's #1 Jingle Singer with commercials for Pizza Hut, Phil Donahue, Black Entertainment Television, Seventh Heaven and many more. In 1987 he was awarded his **First of Five consecutive Washington Area Music Association (WAMMIE) Awards (3 for Best Jazz Vocalist & 2 for Best Inspirational Vocalist).**

In 1990 the DC Public Schools asked **Willie** to join the Drug Prevention division as a Project Coordinator to develop a program using arts and music to attract youth to seek positive alternatives to drugs and violence. The program was called **"Positive Images"** and became an overnight success, winning awards from The Department of Education and Blue Cross/Blue Shield. It was from this platform that he started speaking, first to young inner city students, then to teachers and administrators.

In 1991 **Willie** started speaking full time and his rise has been phenomenal. He is now the **President of the prestigious National Capitol Speakers Association, has spoken to over a million people nationally and internationally, is the host of the syndicated radio show "The Magnificent Motivational Minute" and the author of the exciting new book "It Only Takes A Minute To Change Your Life!"**

A DREAMER who is also a DOER ! The Powerful, The Passionate, The Persuasive, The Phenomenal ... The InspirTainer ... <u>WILLIE JOLLEY!</u>

OTHER PRODUCTS

Motivational Tapes

Don't Be Intimidated By The Obstacles (Live!) $9.99
Change Your Thinking & Change Your Life +How To Develop Diamonds!
(2 Cassettes) $19.99
The Les Brown Dream Team featuring Willie Jolley & You've Got To Have
A Dream $9.99
Turbo-Charge Your Speaking Career: How To Go From Unknown To Known
In A Year! $9.99

Youth/Young Adult

The Real Deal About The Three Little Pigs (Children's Motivator) $9.99
Dare 2 Dream . . . Dare 2 Win! (The #1 Youth & Young Adult Motivational
Program) $9.99

Music Products

We Wish You A Jolley Christmas (The Christmas Album) $9.99
Sunny (The Jazz Album) $9.99
Blessed Assurance (The Inspirational Music Album) $9.99

Video Products

You've Got To Have A Dream $29.99
The National Anthem - Sung by Willie Jolley & Jane Herlong $9.99

Books

It Only Takes A Minute To Change Your Life! *$24.95*
It Only Takes A Minute To Change Your Life! (Audio version of the book -
2 cassettes) $19.95

Please add $5.00 Shipping & Handling

For more information contact:
InspirTainment Plus
P.O. Box 55459
Washington, DC 20040
800-487-8899 • 202-723-8863

8

Only The **BEST**

ON CUFF LINKS

AND LUCK

BY

SCOTT McKAIN

SUCCESS

ON CUFF LINKS
AND LUCK

SCOTT MCKAIN

With the accelerator pressed to the floor, I sped to Springfield, Illinois. I was excited, for not only was it an important presentation, many of my friends in the speaking business were going to be there, too.

Arriving at the hotel about 9:30 in the evening, I dashed up to my room to quickly unpack so I could join my colleagues for a drink. As I pulled my shirt from the suitcase, my heart sank. This was just a quick overnight trip, so I had packed only one shirt. Unfortunately, I realized it was a shirt with French cuffs...and my cuff links were on my night stand in my bedroom in Indianapolis!

I immediately had a new priority! Let's face it — floppy cuffs do not make a good impression on a room full of business leaders!

I ran to the hotel's gift shop. Closed.

Across the street I scurried to the Hilton's gift shop. Closed as well.

Back to my hotel and the bell stand. "Where," I gasped to the bell captain, "can I buy cuff links tonight?"

"Tonight? At 9:30 in Springfield? You gotta be kidding!"

I immediately realized I was not about to receive Nordstrom-quality, "whatever-it-takes" service.

"W-e-e-l-l-l," the bell captain said, stroking his chin, "your only shot is on the other side of town. Wal-Mart and Target are in a shopping center over there, and they are open until ten."

"Oh, you'll have to hurry. It is about a twenty-minute drive."

I glanced at my watch and saw the awful truth: *9:40!*

Back to my car, the accelerator back to the floor, I raced down the streets of the Illinois state capitol. I ran two red lights, and felt like Mario Andretti on a couple of turns.

I made it to Wal-Mart in fifteen minutes. Sprinting into the store, I could hear the announcement being made, "Five minutes until closing, Wal-Mart shoppers!"

Standing guard at the entrance to every Wal-Mart is the "greeter." Most often, you will find a wonderfully friendly senior citizen. Occasionally, however, you will get the person with whom no one else in the store wants to work. That was the case at the Springfield Wal-Mart on this night.

Nonchalantly, he drawled, "Well, good evenin'. Welcome to Wal-Mart."

"Cuff links!", I shouted. "Where are the cuff links?"

"Do what?" was his response.

"I said," repeating myself slowly and distinctly, "where are the cuff links?"

"Hmmm," he pondered, "you know, we don't have

right many people askin' for cuff links in here."

Time was wasting.

"Maybe," he advised, "you should try over there in jewelry."

Moving like a running back around tacklers, I dodged shopping carts and displays to maneuver to the two women supervising the jewelry department.

"Do you have cuff links?" I screeched.

Their facial expressions told me all I needed to know about their inventory.

I had one more shot, for Target was a block away.

As I dashed in the store, I heard the announcement, "It's ten o'clock, Target shoppers. Bring your final purchases to the register now."

I must have looked desperate, for I caught the sympathetic eye of a checkout clerk.

"CUFF LINKS!", I exclaimed.

"Try the men's department!"

I kept running until I skidded up to the counter. Out of breath, I panted the question, "Cuff links?"

Sadly, she shook her head. "No. Is it important?"

"Yes," I said dejectedly. "I have a big speech tomorrow and all I brought was a shirt with cuffs. Thanks, anyway," I said, and turned to walk away.

"Sir?" Her voice was meek as she called me.

"What?", I snapped.

"Well, um, I hope you don't mind my asking, but...*why don't you just buy a new shirt?*"

My response was the same as the guy at Wal-Mart, *"Do what?"*

It dawned on me she was exactly right!

Why not simply buy a new shirt?

Instead of looking for the solution to my problem, I had trapped myself into thinking that only cuff links could make things right.

It occurs to me that many of us do the same thing in business and in life.

Famed speaker and author Jim Rohn says that "most people major in minor things." Most of us would rather spend our time and our lives gathering cuff links than looking for the real solutions to our problems. Most of us would rather place a Band-Aid on the symptom than find the cure.

Why?

The only answer I have been able to find is basic, simplistic, and — I hope — accurate.

It is easier to deal with the trivial than the important.

That means that it is easier to focus on the minor "fixes" and hope. It is much more difficult to make the major effort required to find success.

Gary is a guy I grew up with in my small home town in southern Indiana. He seemed to have nothing. Poor family and poor grades, poor intellect and poor finances

— our class would have probably voted Gary "most likely to be below average."

Yet, he has found one aspect of living that has made him financially independent and successful beyond our, but not his, wildest dreams. He focuses on the big picture.

He decided exactly what he wanted, and lined up all of his limited resources to the accomplishment of his dreams and goals. He is passionate about his work and his family. And, he doesn't have time for anything else. He has, as we would say, been looking for the shirt all along.

I remember being home over a weekend several years ago, and many of the "old gang" from high school were getting together. One of our crowd brought up Gary's name and laughed.

"He'll never go out with us! He's trying to...are you ready for this...get rich!" Laughter engulfed the table and eyes were moist with tears of laughter. Gary, of all people, was working to build a fortune! I will never forget the next line from the guy who was always the class clown: "Gary will be rich when Richard Simmons becomes 'Father of the Year!'" Imagine a group of high school buddies doubled over, pounding a table in hysterics. Imagine who is laughing now.

I am certain you have discovered that there is no single definition to success. It is personal and private, individual and intimate. Success is whatever you define in your mind, heart and soul that you want it to be.

However, along with that definition comes this subtle point: While success is whatever you define it, you <u>must</u> define it to be successful. You cannot be vague or generic — you must precisely and specifically decide what success is for <u>you</u> in order to attain it.

Gary did not have much, but he made what little he had count for all it was worth. He paid the price by not seeing the ball games and concerts that others did — but I am certain he would tell you the reward was worth it.

If you don't make that investment in life, you end up finding cuff links instead of the shirt.

A good friend was telling me about a recent conversation she had with her mother.

"Mom," the conversation went, "we had a great time on vacation in California! We are setting a goal to move there in five years!"

Her mother's response was unexpected. "Oh, honey! For goodness' sake, don't plan your life away. You'll just end up disappointed. You know we're not lucky enough in our family to have all the good things happen to us that you want."

The daughter was devastated that her mother would think like that. She knew her Mom's disappointment with the way that life had turned out, but she could not imagine that her mother would tell her not to plan for the best.

The daughter noticed, however, the important use of

the word "luck" in her mother's vocabulary.

As my friend and I talked, I had a revelation about one of the things that is different between successful people and the folks for whom nothing seems to work.

Define the word "lucky," I asked my friend. Her response was exactly what I expected: *the situation of fortunate circumstances.*

Lou Gehrig in his famous farewell address at Yankee Stadium announced that he was dying, yet he still considered himself, "the luckiest man on the face of the earth." When I recently interviewed Tom Hanks, he told me he believed himself to be "the luckiest guy in the world."

For both of these successful individuals, the opportunity to experience fortunate circumstances made them feel "lucky." Yet, I am certain neither of them would say their success was without hard work, effort, persistence and diligence. They would agree with Abraham Lincoln's oft quoted definition that luck is when "opportunity meets preparedness."

I asked my friend if she would ask her mother the same question. The response her Mom gave also came as no surprise. To her, luck was *the chance happening of events.*

Notice the important difference: to the daughter (by the way, a highly successful corporate executive), luck was finding yourself in fortunate circumstances no matter how you got there. It is feeling blessed to be alive, to enjoy life and to have the opportunity to continue to pursue what you deem to be success.

To the mother, luck was a matter of pure chance.

People became successful because of a roll of the dice, a random selection or a mysterious lottery of life. In the mother's perspective, the planning and goal setting practiced by her daughter was useless, since if you weren't "lucky," you would not achieve it anyway.

Since this conversation happened, I have been amazed to note how many folks feel that the outcome of their lives is dependent upon mere chance. Perhaps that's why they buy the extra lottery ticket, take a trip to Vegas and sit home and watch television every night.

One of the real mysteries of life is why good fortune seems to smile so easily on some people and not on others. Yet, in most situations, doesn't it seem as though most people really get out of life what they put into it? I saw a bumper sticker the other day that said, "Life is like a Coke bottle. No deposit. No return."

The people who wait on luck are seldom — if ever — successful because they aren't making the deposits that life requires for return. What will it take for you to really "get lucky?" What effort is necessary for you to find yourself in a lifetime of fortunate circumstances?

Maybe you need to <u>learn</u> more. Let's face it, in today's changing world, continuing education is a necessity.

Maybe you need to <u>think</u> more. When was the last time you sat down with just a pen and paper for an hour and *thought?* Few of us have experienced that exercise for quite a while. I believe that most of us are so busy "doing" that we spend little time thinking about what it is that we are doing.

Maybe you need to <u>be</u> more. One of the great challenges in life is to make the commitment and effort necessary to be the kind of person who deserves on-going fortunate circumstances.

Earl Nightingale used to say that no one would sit in front of a stove and say, "First give me some heat. THEN I'll give you some wood." Yet, for many people, that is precisely the deal they are trying to make with life.

For years I dismissed my grandfather's advice as a meaningless cliché: "The harder I work, the luckier I get." Now, I realize what seemed to be trite is, instead, profound.

For you to get "Only the Best" from life and find the success you want, I suggest you focus on the big things that are important. Do not waste your time with cuff links when the shirt is there for you. Make the investments you need in education, effort, time and resources so that fortunate circumstances are the rule rather than the exception for the rest of your life.

SCOTT MCKAIN

As a professional speaker, seminar leader, and consultant, Scott McKain has received rave reviews over the past 15 years. With topics ranging from customer service and communication, achievement and motivation, Scott can tailor his programs to any audience with a blend of cutting-edge information and  sharp humor. He provides solid information in an entertaining package—a winning combination for any audience.

Scott has given presentations for audiences which range in size from 20 to 10,000+, for international companies, state organizations, and non-profits. He has satisfied each one by working with them to customize his presentation to their specific needs, adding a touch of wit to send the message home.

Scott grew up in rural America, and brings his knowledge of "real people" to each presentation he makes. His leadership skills developed early—he was elected a National Officer of FFA, an organization of over half a million members, before graduating from college. Other honors include being on several presidential committees, being named in "Who's Who in the Midwest" and a Jaycees "Outstanding Young Men in America." In addition to his speaking career, Scott also has a successful commentary show syndicated to over 80 stations across the US, Canada, and Australia.

OTHER PRODUCTS

Just Say YES! A Step Up To Success! • *The seven cassette, fourteen day program to personal achievement that started it all! As seen on national TV!!! Learn the importance of values and priorities, goal setting and communication, and the "Six Steps Up To Success!" Sold on national television for $79.95 . . . special price for Only The Best readers:* $49.95

Just Say YES! A Step up To Success • *The hot-selling book based on the audio cassette album. With a foreword by baseball hall of famer, Jim Palmer! A must read!!! In bookstores for $29.95 . . . special Only The Best price:* $19.95

Just Say YES! A Step Up To Success! • *A full-hour video of the best of the entertainment and enlightenment of Scott McKain.*
(VHS format only) $19.95

Dragonslayers! • *Scott's first audio program. Recorded live and in-studio. The cassettes of humor and information on change, humor and relationships. (Limited quantities available.)* $19.95

Single audio tape of fun with Scott! Laugh and learn. some of the best of Scott's classic humor and some new fun with a master of message and merriment! $10.00

SAVE!!! get the whole package for only $99.95

Visa, Master Card, and American Express accepted.
Please include $4.50 for shipping and handling.

For more information contact:
McKain Performance Group
P. O. Box 24800
Indianapolis, IN 46224
800-297-5844
317-875-0708
FAX 317-875-0038

9

Only The BEST

JUMPING

BY

CHRIS CLARKE-EPSTEIN

SUCCESS

JUMPING

CHRIS CLARKE-EPSTEIN

My son Paul called the other day. "Mom," he said, "You'll never guess what I did this weekend. I went bungee cord jumping."

My reply was swift. "Paul, I'm so glad that you called to tell me that you *went* bungee jumping rather than that you were *thinking about* going bungee cord jumping!" This is not what a mom expects to hear, out of the blue. Actually I don't know why I was surprised. This is the same kid who rigged a Super 8 movie camera to record his flying leaps off the garage roof into a snow bank.

After my pulse rate returned to normal, my curiosity asserted itself. "Tell me about it."

"I was surprised," he said. "They required payment before you climbed up the tower. And the guy was really emphatic about the fact that there were no refunds. He said he didn't care if you jumped off or climbed down, your money was theirs."

He continued, "When you got to the top, they

strapped you into the harness, showed you how the equipment was checked and rechecked and then you had to jump off."

"You know Paul", I said, "I've always dreamed about parachuting. I can envision myself floating down, I just can't see myself jumping out of the plane. I guess someone would have to push me."

"No Mom, at least with bungee jumping, it doesn't work that way. They won't push you. You have to jump on your own. In fact the guy told me, count to three, don't think, just jump. And I did. It was great! "

Paul's story that day reminded me that all the successful people I know, have taken risks along their paths to achievement.

Most of us aren't comfortable with risk. Even thinking about risk makes many of us nervous. Being presented with a risk often paralyzes us into inaction. What irony. The only way to improve is to try something different. The only way to try something different is to take a chance. Chance implies an equal possibility of success and failure. The success doesn't worry us, the failure does. Paul seems to be working on Master's level risk courses and getting good grades. All the necessary elements for effective risk taking were there to be learned while bungee jumping.

Paul had to pay whether he jumped or not. He needed to make a decision to act. Life carries very few certainties, so if you wait until an opportunity comes along that has a money-back guarantee, you could wait for a very long time. When successful people approach risk, they know they have to make their commitment to action rather than success. My friend and author of *Stick To It!*, C. Leslie Charles said, "Success always begins with a thought but it is achieved through action."

Remember when Billy Jean King played tennis against Bobby Riggs? We had a party at our house to watch what was billed as the battle of the sexes. To write this I had to ask my husband, Frank, "Who won?" (it was Billie Jean). So much for the sporting event of the 70's. I do, however, remember something Billie Jean said, "Be bold. If you're going to make an error, make it a doozy, and don't be afraid to hit the ball." Most sports stars understand the connection between commitment to action , risk and success. Babe Ruth held the home run record and the strike out record at the same time. Most people convince themselves that they can't hit a home run so they don't bother to try out for the lineup. If they can't win the game, they won't play. The truth is just the opposite. If you don't play, you can't win. Paul made his commitment to action as he handed over his money, no refunds.

(Allow me a personal note about my capacity for risk and action. I KNOW NOTHING ABOUT

SPORTS. I tried for hours to find another example that would make this point better than a sport's metaphor. I couldn't find one. I was willing to drop the whole section until I realized how ironic for me to avoid taking a risk while I was writing about risk! How did I do?)

Paul discovered that before he jumped, he needed to learn about his equipment and get strapped into the harness. Many people have a mistaken perception about risk and preparation. Some believe that if you prepare, it's no longer risk. Others feel that unless you cross every *t* and dot every *i*, it's too much of a risk. Embarking on a risk with no planning would be foolish. Postponing a risk until all the details are ironed out eliminates possibilities. The truth, as it so often does, falls somewhere in the middle.

There is a three step process most risk takers follow. They recall what they already know. Fill any huge gaps of knowledge and listen to their gut. They base their risk taking decisions on a blend of knowledge, past experience and intuition. Because they practice this process often, they get quicker and quicker at it.

To the casual observer, some risk takers seem to be doing no rational pondering at all, just plunging ahead with little regard to life's dangers and realities. That was my initial impression of Paul's flirtation with his mortality, he had obviously acted on impulse. Until I asked how he made his decision and discovered that he had checked with others until he could identify the safest bungee tower in the state, judged his capacity for adventure and acknowledged that this was something he just wanted to do.

(If we were lawyers in a courtroom, I'd be asking the judge for a side-bar. Has the word curiosity popped into your mind at all? Have you noticed that successful people are curious? I believe that their curiosity works to eliminate a possible lack of knowledge at a time when not knowing something or at least having some background information to call on could be critical. Almost everything is risky for a child. They have no way of knowing the rules. They offset their mandatory risk taking, experienced as long division, piano lessons and the first season of Little League for example, with a frenzy of information gathering accomplished by an endless string of "whys". They don't care if they're asking the right question. They know that any question will get them new information to sift through. Maybe you could start asking some interesting questions.)

Paul had to jump off the tower by himself. The element that defines risk best is its requirement of faith. Ultimately to take a risk means to step into the unknown. In her book, *The Last Word*, Carolyn Warner explores the differences between fear and faith. "...if you are afraid of failure you will most likely fail because you are not making a leap into the unknown, but assumed, place of success. Rather, you are making a knee-trembling leap into an expected condition of failure."

I can't remember the first time I heard the expression, "leap of faith," but I understood it right away. Children say good-bye on the first day of kindergarten because they have faith in their parent's promise, "I'll pick you up right after school, honey.". Soldiers follow their leaders into battle on faith. (In my generation some avoided the draft because of a lack of faith in leadership.) Spouses pledge faith in each other. Risk taking requires faith in something.

What do you need to have faith in to be a good risk-taker? Sophia Loren said, "Getting ahead in a difficult profession requires avid faith in yourself." I agree. Successful people believe in them self. This self-belief isn't ego driven, far from it. It is a belief that requires much. They believe that they will do what needs to be done, make mistakes and learn lessons. That process is often called growth. They have faith in their ability to grow.

Faith in yourself isn't enough. Successful risk-takers have faith in others. They believe that, by and large, other people wish them well and will help when called upon. Some see this as a naive point of view and enjoy regaling listeners with stories of times when others have failed them.

These stories, which often contain fine drama and heated dialogue, get a response from the risk-taker of, "Oh, that hasn't been my experience." They have a whole warehouse of stories, examples and personal experience that they can call on to prove the opposite is true. No one succeeds by them self.

(Last pause in the narrative. Does it occur to you that our successful people sound a lot like optimists? They do and they are. They have learned the power of expectations. What you expect out of people is usually what you get. It doesn't seem to make a difference - expect a lousy day and the universe will oblige. Expect a miracle and you'd be surprised how often one happens.)

Their faith doesn't end with others either. They have faith in something beyond themselves and others. They call it many different things, God, Allah, Jesus, a Higher Power, but they all carry the same message. There is a purpose to each of our lives. We exist for something more than ourselves. Just as a child will jump off the side of a swimming pool into water way over their head because of their parent's outstretched arms, every successful person I know believes there is a force that operates in their life. It is that force that guides, sustains and comforts them during life's biggest risk-taking adventures.

Faith is what ultimately allows us to step into the unknown. To paraphrase Marilyn Ferguson, in her book, *The Aquarian Conspiracy*, "...it's not so much that we fear change or that we like the status quo. It's that we dislike the transition. We're like Linus standing in front of the dryer waiting for his blanket.". We, like Linus, fear the not-knowing. Ultimately, Linus lets go of his blanket because he has faith in his mom. What is the faith that allows you to leap?

I'm still not ready to take a bungee jump. But risks come in many different packages. Some people spend their whole lives trying to avoid them. They wake up one day realizing that because they never took a chance, they never got to win. I can hear Bette Midler's voice as I write, singing *The Rose*. Remember the lines? "It's the heart afraid of dying that never learns to live." I've always loved that song, find a copy and listen to its powerful message.

All the successful people I know have taken risks along their path to achievement. I think they would all agree with Rosalynn Carter (at least on this), "You must accept that you might fail; then, if you do your best and still don't win, at least you can be satisfied that you've tried. If you don't accept failure as a possibility, you don't set high goals, you don't branch out, you don't try – you don't take the risk." And if you don't take the risk you can never be a success.

Try an experiment. For the next several days ask people

to remember the big risks they've taken in their lives. Ask them what happened as a result of those risks. I'll make a wager about their answers. Those who recount little risks, minor victories, big failures and can't articulate any lessons learned from either will be people you wouldn't identify as successful. Those who can go on and on, regaling you with stories of their leaps into the unknown, spectacular crashes, incredible wins and lessons they have carried for the rest of their lives, will be the ones you have always admired.

They weren't bungee jumps, but I can recall several times in my life when it certainly felt as though I was up on a tower looking down a very long distance. Sometimes I was really scared. At other times I was exhilarated. I can hardly figure out where I got the courage to jump. I can barely remember checking my qualifications and resources. I do recall the feeling of faith, sometimes in myself, more often in others and always in something that would show me the way out of failure if I needed it. I jumped.

Chris Clarke-Epstein

Chris Clarke-Epstein, CSP has done many things in her life - from successfully managing a 7 million dollar sales territory, raising 2 mostly economically self-sufficient children and, since 1984, building a thriving speaking, training and consulting business.

Her mother claims that Chris gave her first speech at age 6, when she was caught lining up the neighborhood children, collecting their nickels and promising them a narrated tour of her newborn brother. These days, Chris delivers over 100 speaking and training programs a year helping people learn faster, work better and laugh harder. Her programs on building effective teams, increasing personal creativity and thriving during change energize audiences with a powerful blend of sound research, practical experience and infectious enthusiasm. Her clients, from Fortune 500 Companies to State and National Associations, often pay her the highest compliments - they bring her back again and recommend her to others.

Chris is an active members of the American Society for Training and Development and serves on the Board of Directors of the National Speakers Association. She has been recognized for excellence by both. In July of 1993, Chris earned the Certified Speaking Professional designation from NSA, a designation she shares with fewer than 300 other CSP's in the world.

Chris is the author of two books and has recorded several tape series that allow people to take her ideas and humor home with them. Her stories of real people living in the real world encourage people to re-evaluate their own ability to have the life they want.

OTHER PRODUCTS

Simple Encounters: Stories of Life, Laughter and Livelihood $12.50
You'll read this collection of warm, witty and touching essays over and over again

Putting Humor To Work $16.00
The perfect tape to keep in your car. It's guaranteed to lift your spirits!

So, Who Motivates The Motivator? *$12.00*
You'll listen to this tape more than once to remind yourself of the 5 steps to a self-charged life.

Whatever Happened To Ward, June, Wally and the Beav? $12.00
Listen to this tape to learn how manage change creatively.

The Four Basic Guilt Groups $12.00
For women only, a tape to help you lessen guilt and increase action

Putting Humor To Work, the Video $40.00
Watch a live presentation guaranteed to teach laugh filled strategies to even the humor impaired!

Can't decide, order Simple Encounters, Putting Humor To Work, the video and 3 tapes of your choice for the very special price of $ 70.00

Please add $3.00 Shipping & Handling

To order or for more information about Chris's books, tapes, speeches and training sessions contact:

SPEAKING!
P.O. Box 37
Wausau, WI 54402-0037
715-842-2467 • fax: 715-848-9463
e-mail: ChrisCE@aol.com

10

Only The BEST

LIVE LIKE YOUR LIFE DEPENDS ON IT

BY

MARK SANBORN

SUCCESS

LIVE LIKE YOUR LIFE DEPENDS ON IT

MARK SANBORN

You can learn important lessons about life in some unusual places. I had an insight about the secret of successful living while eating soup.

I was delighted to discover that a new restaurant in my neighborhood had corn chowder on the menu. Corn chowder is one of my all-time favorites, so I ordered a bowl. When it arrived, I was disappointed. It just wasn't very good corn chowder. The reason was simple: there wasn't much corn in it. You can't rave about corn chowder that doesn't have enough corn in it.

That's the way life is, too. You can't rave about a life that hasn't had much living in it. Just like corn chowder, the secret of successful living is to put more life into it! Success is about living life fully, not adding minutes to each day.

Many lead lives of monotony and dullness punctuated by brief periods of excitement and fulfillment. Bruno Gouvy died June 15, 1990 while attempting an extreme snowboard descent in Chamonix, France. His death was tragic, but the words he shared about risk and his philosophy of life live on:

"In western civilization we lead very structured lives. I think laws are good—they hold society together. But I also think that from time to time we need to touch a more primitive instinct. On the cliff face you are your own authority. There is no policeman, judge or lawyer to give you permission. You must decide for yourself.

Sure, there is a chance I might be killed. But in exchange, I have such a powerful sense of being alive. It's a bargain. I look at the risk, I take every step to minimize it, and in exchange for this little risk, I receive such a huge joy in living. Without risk, the sun is just the sun, grass is just grass. With risk, common things have incredible freshness."

I, too, desire to lead a life of excitement and significance, interrupted only by the fewest possible moments of monotony. While the risks you and I view as acceptable vary, the point remains the same: It isn't about what happens each day, but rather what you make happen—or make of what happens.

In the movie "Dead Poets Society," Robin Williams played the role of a teacher who enriched the lives of his students by teaching them to understand the importance of Carpe Diem—seize the day. So Carpe Diem! Make a concerted effort to seize the day and fill it with big chunks of life.

The quality of your life is a choice! You can feel fully alive, and joyful most of the time, not just some of the time. The key is to live like your life depends on it. But how?

To live fully, we need a personal philosophy. Philosophy is the pursuit of wisdom and answers the question, "How should we live?" Personal philosophy, therefore, answers the question, "How should I live?" Here are five principles to integrate into your personal philosophy.

Live Purposefully

Why do you get out of bed in the morning?

I've asked that question to dozens of audiences over the past decade. I usually get only two responses. The first is, *"I have to."* That response suggests a vague sense of obligation or compulsion. Truth is, however, that most people don't have to get out of bed in the morning. If they stayed there long enough, somebody would come to check up on them!

The second response is more basic: *"I have to go to the bathroom."* Does this explain much about the motivational level of some of the people you work with? You:

"Why did you come into work today?" Them: "Oh, I got up about 6:00 this morning to go to the bathroom and decided as long as I was up I would come to the office to see what was going on....." Some people are more motivated by their bladder than by their beliefs.

So why do *you* get out of bed each morning? Dr. Charles Garfield has done important research on peak performance. He's found of the six attributes that create it, mission is at the top of the list. Your mission is the reason *why* for *what* you do each day. Purposeful people have powerful reasons for getting out of bed in the morning.

Live With 60/60 Vision

My friend Brian O'Malley is an extremely interesting guy. Today he is a speaker who shares his experiences as a world traveler, mountain climber, and adventurer. Prior to that he spent eight years in emergency medicine. It's sobering to learn that he's been with over 250 people in the final minute of their lives. The important insight, Brian says, is that none of those people's last words were, "I wish I had spent more time in the office!" The last 60 seconds of life, is a time of stunningly clear perspective

Roger Mellot is a therapist and speaker who authored an excellent tape entitled "The Courage To See Clearly." He explains that when his father was given 60 days to live because of a serious illness, his dad's perspective changed dramatically. He stopped doing things that he didn't enjoy or felt weren't important and focused on making the most of what he thought were his final days.

Wouldn't it be helpful, Roger suggests, if we could gain the same window on the world as someone with only 60 days left to live? Wouldn't that enable us to live fuller, richer, and more honest lives?

These examples are hopeful, not morose—if we understand the lessons within. And the lessons aren't about dying, they're about living.

Combining these two concepts results in what I call 60/60 Vision. You can use this technique to see with clarity what is really important in your life.

In the final moments of your life, will you have regrets, or will you celebrate the fact that while you were alive you really lived? When it comes down to a few accomplishments that bring ultimate life significance, what will they be for you?

If you lived life with 60/60 vision:

Would your communication with others be more honest?
How would you approach your work?

Who would you spend more time with?
Who would you decide to spend less time with (or
no time at all)?
What would you stop worrying about?
What would you strive to be remembered for?
What would you do each day to maximize enjoyment?
What contributions would you strive to make?

Then why not live your life that way now? Why wait
for the final countdown? You and I may never get to
know when we're living our final sixty—days or seconds—
and even if we do find out, it will be too late to change
very much. The only time is the present.

Psalm 90:12 says, "Teach us to number our days aright,
that we may gain heart of wisdom." (NIV) To live fully
and with significance, look at your life with 60/60 vision.

Live A High Performance Lifestyle

It is hard to live a high performance life in a low performance body. Creating a high performance lifestyle isn't
easy, but neither is it as hard as many assume.

To begin, make sure that you're getting at least 30
minutes or more of moderate-intensity physical activity
most days of the week. A panel convened by the Centers
for Disease Control and Prevention and the American
College of Sports Medicine made this recommendation

in early 1994. The panel believes that adults who exercise at this level will receive significant health benefits.

The journal Nature also found that growth factors in the brain—compounds responsible for the brain's health—can be controlled by exercise. Exercisers live longer, score higher on tests of mental function and this indicates the importance of physical activity in the aging process. Building biceps may really boost brainpower, too, according to the somewhat controversial new research.

And yet despite these benefits, only one in every five Americans exercise regularly. Of those who don't exercise, 51% say it is because they don't have the time. If you fall into that excuse category, you owe it to yourself to *make* the time.

Next, minimize those substances that affect your energy negatively. Caffeine, alcohol, cigarettes, and sugar can confuse the body, especially when ingested close to bedtime. More than two to three cups of coffee per day can create an addiction that results in needing large quantities of coffee just to experience normal energy levels. The body actually stops producing its natural energy chemicals.

Some other ideas that both study and personal experience have found helpful for maintaining higher energy levels: Eat more frequently. Light healthy snacking—

fruits, vegetables, not candy—provides the body with an ongoing source of fuel between meals. Healthy snacking between meals prevents over-eating at regular meal times.

And importantly, stay hydrated. Drink lots of water. Water plays a critical role in digestion and nutrition; you can think of it as the oil that keeps your metabolic engine lubricated. Instead of coffee, I keep a large glass of water on my desk. The urge to sip coffee has been replaced with water and my energy level and general well-being have improved.

Live With Disciplined Spontaneity

There is a Samurai maxim that says, "To know and to act are one and the same." The Samurai believed that you and I don't really know something until we use it, that if we have information and we're not applying the information, true understanding hasn't taken place.

It takes discipline to live fully. But spontaneity is important too. Here's how to develop both.

Once each day for the rest of your life do something tough or challenging, not because you want to, but because it's good for you and it proves to you that you can do what needs to be done.

My first job after college took me to a small town in

Wisconsin. It was there that I took up distance running. I ran from nine to eleven miles every day. Friends sometimes said, "If you run nine to eleven miles a day, you must really enjoy running." In actuality, I didn't always enjoy it. When it was cold or raining, or when I was tired after a day at the office, I didn't enjoy doing the roadwork.

Why did I do it? Running became my mechanism of proving to me that I was in control: that I could do what I needed to do; that I had control, not over just my mind, but over my body as well.

I'm not suggesting that running should be your primary mechanism for developing discipline (although it can be a pretty good one). I am advocating that you find a sport or other activity in your life that you can do each day as a means for developing discipline.

Secondly, every day for the rest of your life, do something just for the pure fun of it. I don't believe that we should delay joy. The only thing that we're sure of is today. I have a magnet on my refrigerator that says, *"Eat dessert first. Life is too tentative."*

The key to a balanced life is discipline coupled with spontaneity. Too much, or too little of either can be detrimental to living like your life depends on it.

Live Beyond Self-Actualization

The pastor of my church is a pretty hip guy. I bought my Harley Davidson from him (he believes that if Jesus were alive today, He would ride a Harley). Dr. Bob Beltz has written several books, but one of my favorites is "The Solomon Syndrome" (Revell). You may be familiar with Abraham Maslow's hiearchy of needs (Motivation and Personality, 1954). Maslow believed that self-actualization was a person's highest need. But Bob points out, *"In his later years, Maslow recognized that self-actualization was not the highest objective of human development and motivation. He began to talk in terms of self-transcendence, by which he meant that the ultimate objective of life was to live for something greater than ourselves."* He was on target.

Bob believes, as I do, that we were designed to be what he calls "God- actualized." I don't know what your spiritual beliefs are (and you may be recoiling at my mention of this topic), but I do know that living only for self is a dead-end street.

Beyond self-actualization means living to be of service to others: family, friends, the community and—if you're a believer—God. There is significance that can only be experienced when we go beyond ourselves to be of service to others.

Relationships count. Albert Einstein once said that if

there is a reason we exist, it must be for each other. Bubba Bechtol is a speaking colleague and friend from Pensacola, Florida who lost everything in a hurricane in 1995. He wrote me these profound words, "I have lost every material thing I ever had in my life and found friends I never knew I had—friends are better....."

Checklist for a Successful Day

Our lives are the sum total of the choices we make and the things we do each day. That's why I've developed my checklist for a successful day. I'll share it with you in the hope, that this will become a check list that you will use for making every day, extraordinary.

Did I tell or show someone that I loved them?
Did I compliment or praise someone I live or work with today?
Did I read a book or listen to a tape that stimulated my thinking?
Did I increase my skill in my profession?
Did I do something for good health?
Am I closer to my goals than when I woke up this morning?
Did I do anything tough or challenging to build discipline?
Did I do something just for the pure joy of it?
Have I taken time to reflect on the lessons of the day?
Have I planned for another successful day tomorrow?

If you can answer yes to most of these questions, you have created a day of uncommon success.

George Santayana said, "There is no cure for birth and death save to enjoy the interval." Live fully—your life depends on it.

MARK SANBORN, CSP, CPAE

Because of his ability to educate and entertain simultaneously, Mark Sanborn is known internationally as the high content speaker who motivates. Mark presents an average of 90 programs yearly on leadership, teambuilding, customer service and mastering change.

He is the author of Teambuilt: Making Teamwork Work, Sanborn On Success, sixteen videos and four audio training programs. His video, "Teambuilding: How to Manage and Motivate People" was the #2 bestselling business video in America.

In 1993 he was selected by ECI/Westcott Communications as one of 11 Masters On Motivation for their business television series. Presentations magazine featured him in the article, "Masters of the Microphone." In 1995, Mark earned the C.S.P. designation (Certified Speaking Professional) and was honored with the C.P.A.E. award (Council of Peers Award of Excellence) from the National Speakers Association.

Mark offers speeches, seminars, books, audios and videos for both organizational and personal development. Mark's most requested presentations include:

The Fred Factor: Reinventing Your Business & Life
The 10 Commandments of Customer Service
Mastering Change
The 3R's of Leadership
Teambuilding: Making Teamwork Work

OTHER PRODUCTS

How To Live The American Dream (one hour motivational video) $99
How To Manage Your Time, Energy & Relationships (2 audios) $20
The Fred Factor: Reinventing Your Business & Your Life Through Personal Leadership (audio) $10
Mastering Change (2 audio cassettes) $25
Mastering Change (2 one hour videos) $199
Mastering Change (2 audio cassettes) $25
Teambuilding: How To Manage & Motivate People (4 audios) $49
Teambuilding: How To Manage & Motivate People (2 videos) $249
High Impact Leadership (4 audios) $49
High Impact Leadership (3 videos) $249
Teambuilding workbooks .... $5 ea.
High Impact Leadership workbooks .... $5 ea.
Empowerment: Unleashing the Potential of Performance (video) $159
Teambuilt: Making Teamwork Work (book) $12.95
Sanborn On Success (book) $8.95

Please add $5.00 Shipping & Handling

To order or for more information about Mark's books, tapes, speeches and training sessions contact:

Sanborn & Associates, Inc.
677 S. Williams
Denver, CO 80209
(800) 650-3343 • Fax (303) 777 3045
internet: MarkSpeaks@aol.com
web page: http://www.expertcenter.com/members/marksanborn

11

Only The BEST

ATTITUDE: THE POWER TO SUCCEED

BY

KEITH HARRELL

SUCCESS

ATTITUE: THE POWER TO SUCCEED

Your Attitude Today Determines Your Success Tomorrow...

KEITH HARRELL

Attitude. As far back as I can remember, I've heard about the importance of a positive attitude and the effect it would have in my life. I heard it all through school, from Little League to college basketball, and from my days at IBM up to owning my own business.

Think back. How many times in your life have you heard about having a positive attitude? Although attitude is a powerful word that plays an important role in everyone's life, it is ironic that most people don't know its meaning—or its impact on their lives. What, then, is attitude?

The dictionary defines the word *attitude* as "one's feelings or mood toward things or people." Well, congratulations. Based on this definition, we all have an attitude, because we all have feelings about something or someone.

I have a different, one-word definition of attitude: *life.* That's right, attitude is the difference-maker in life. It's a treasure that lies within you. A positive attitude is the key that jump-starts your life. Attitude dictates whether you're living life or life is living you. Attitude determines whether you are *on* the way or *in* the way.

Think about it: There are billions of people in the world, and there's one thing that every one of us has— attitude. The good news is, you don't have to buy it. The other news—not necessarily bad—is that if you want an attitude that works for you, that improves the quality of your life and enables you to accomplish your dreams, you have to work for it. It's not something you can just sit around and wait for.

Over the years, I've attended many seminars, read many books, listened to many tapes and interviewed many successful people on the subject of self-development— only to discover that nothing comes close to the power of a positive attitude. In fact, the most valuable assets you possess are your attitude toward yourself and your attitude toward life. As you will learn as you read through this chapter, what matters is not how much you know about maintaining a positive attitude, but how well and how consistently you put that knowledge to use.

How you use that knowledge is more vital than you may think. Recent studies link our thoughts—positive or negative—to our immune systems. Scientific research indicates that our minds and bodies act on each other in ways we had not foreseen. Positive attitudes seem to have a beneficial effect on our health and longevity.

Happily, many researchers believe—and I wholeheartedly agree with them—that optimism or positive attitudes are not a result of genetics and heredity; but, with proper training, an optimist can be made.

I'm a very positive person—I choose to see myself, others and all situations from a positive perspective. The material you're about to read isn't just a lot of cheerleading. If you want a positive attitude, you're going to need to be committed enough to work for it.

Each of us can decide to change our primary attitude— all it requires is a little checking and testing. Most of us go to a physician or dentist once or twice a year just to stay aware of our health and to maintain our wellness. Most of us do the same for our cars; we take them to a quick-lube place every few thousand miles. Sadly, many of us don't give our personal well-being that same type of attention.

According to Martin Seligman, a notable psychologist at the University of Pennsylvania, optimist—individuals with a positive attitude—are more successful than similarly talented pessimists. His research also indicates that negative attitudes can be changed into positive attitudes.

Seligman's study has shown that our attitudes—positive or negative—affect how we succeed or fail. *Executive Female Magazine* states that two studies have shown that life insurance agents with optimistic attitudes sold more than their pessimistic colleagues. Pessimists blamed failed sales attempts on themselves, which lowered their self-esteem, which led to lower sales volumes. Optimists, rather than taking the rejections personally, had logical reasons why prospects did not buy policies. Optimists not only sold 37% more than pessimists, they remained on the job longer.

The last decade has produced mounting research that points to the fact that positive thinking aids in the healing process. British researchers have evidence showing a tie between negative emotions and illness. The same study demonstrates a connection between positives attitudes and good health.

These studies are the tip of the iceberg when it comes to the power our minds have over our bodies. So positive thinking isn't just the gushing of a naive person—there are sound reasons for you to develop a consistently positive attitude.

One of the great things about a positive attitude, is it doesn't work just for you, it doesn't work just for those around you, it works for everybody.

Ever since I became a professional speaker and trainer, a lot of my work has been with corporations. Managers have invited me to speak to their sales forces, their office staffs or their management groups. But over the last several years, there has been a change in the tone of the invitations.

In my first year, the invitations were something like this: "Keith, we're going for a record year and I really want to keep my people pumped up. I'd like for you to help us raise our attitudes another notch."

During the next two years, the tone was not nearly as upbeat. The invitations were more like this: "Keith, we've got a real morale problem. Our people are more worried about their futures than their work. Frankly, I have to do something. Keith, I know you can help us and we're ready to get started. What can you do to help?"

In two short years, the workplace had changed dramatically. Companies were either "downsizing" or "rightsizing," "smartsizing," or "capsizing," according to whether your job was one of these eliminated. Thousands of people who thought their lives were secure through retirement were suddenly vulnerable. Some were unemployed, and those who remained wondered when their turn would come.

It's the kind of circumstance that can defeat you...if you let circumstance dictate your life.

That's what happened to a lot of people. But for others, this circumstance was just one more step toward getting where they wanted to go.

NEGATIVE SELF-TALK

Here are some important questions that only you can answer:

Are you destroying your attitude with your own internal conversation? Are you limiting your performance because of negative self-talk? You may be asking, what is self-talk? How can it limit me if it's just talk? If it's that important, how can you change negative self-talk to positive self-talk?

Self-talk—that incessant little voice we listen to all day long—acts like a seed, in that it programs our brains and affects our behavior. The good news is that the information in our brains can be reprogrammed. So why don't we take a closer look at what we're saying to ourselves and start reprogramming for personal and professional success? Below are a few examples of positive and negative self-talk I have overheard. As you read these, compare them to your own conversations.

NEGATIVE SELF-TALK	POSITIVE SELF-TALK
I am not artistic.	I am creative in my own way.
I just know it won't work.	I know it will work, because I've got what it takes.
Mondays are not good days for me.	Every day is an opportunity.

BENEFITS OF POSITIVE SELF-TALK

An important element of maintaining a positive attitude is self-talk.

Self-talk gives you the capability to control your destiny through the most accessible power at your disposal: controlling what you say to yourself. It sounds too simple and to good to be true. It is simple, but the truth is, changing old habits and patterns is difficult. You must be committed and very determined to keep your self-talk positive. You need to monitor your self-talk every second of the day. Don't expect to be perfect 100% of the time. Some of that self-talk you're spouting is rooted in decades of practice. Stay committed and determined, but be patient and kind to yourself. Otherwise, you'll be adding more negative thoughts to your self-talk.

The benefits of altering your self-talk are unlimited.

If you're willing to work at it, what you want is what you can get.

Another important element of maintaining a positive attitude:

AFFIRMATIONS

An affirmation is a positive statement of truth. To affirm is to make firm in your mind. It is stating something to be true regardless of all evidence to the contrary. It is a type of mental activity used for building consciousness or awareness. It lifts you out of false thinking. An affirmation contains the elements of your belief, attitude, and motivation.

An affirmation is made up of words—words charged with power, conviction, and faith. Everytime you speak, atoms of your body are affected; their rate of vibration is either raised or lowered. The purpose of an affirmation is to impress the subconscious mind, for what is impressed is expressed. This process involves repetition, feeling, and imaging.

Repetition is very important. By repeating the affirmation, you send a positive response to your subconscious, which, as we discussed, accepts whatever you tell it. When done properly, this triggers positive feelings that, in turn, drive action. Imaging is the process that allows you to see it in your mind; once you can see it in you mind, you'll be closer to achieving it in your life.

Affirmations, repeated several times each day, every day, serve to reprogram your subconscious with positive thinking. Remember, too, that as positive thinking takes hold in your mind, your body responds accordingly. If you're having trouble accepting this concept, which has considerable scientific evidence and research confirming it, think about this somewhat ordinary occurrence: blushing. Many of us blush (trust me, some of us still do) when we are embarrassed. Sometimes it might be because of something we hear or see. We haven't exerted ourselves to the point that blood rushes to leave our faces flushed—it's the mere thought or sight of a situation that causes this physiological reaction. If we have this kind of physical display from the thought, why is it difficult to believe that a positive thought would affect our bodies in a beneficial way? Research also shows that the simple act of smiling causes your brain to release a stream of chemicals that make you feel good. The best things in life really are free. SMILE!

Affirmations not only help you to keep positive, they also stir the power within you. This power within you needs to be coached and guided to maximize your performance. No one can motivate you but *you*—it comes from the inside out. Thus, we each need to use our own internal coach to guide the power within us. Your attitude coach is a coach that lives within you, always seeking to confirm a positive action or event.

CREATING YOUR OWN AFFIRMATIONS

The statements you design for your affirmations must be positive and in the present tense. Do not use words such as "try," "wish," or "hope." These are all acceptable words, but not in your affirmations. Your statement is affirming and confirming that what you want to become the truth is already the truth—a done deal. Do not say, "I'll try to learn," or "I hope I can be a better person," etc. Instead, declare "I am learning all the material presented to me in class," or "each day I am a better, stronger, more balanced person."

You want to affirm what you want to be true. But, steer clear of fantasies. I am a really, really positive thinker, but if one of my affirmations was, "I am the CEO of Delta Air Lines, and I know more about the airline industry than anyone in the world, I would be in for a real let down. First of all the CEO of Delta Air Lines is Ron Allen. It's also highly unlikely I'd be the CEO of an airline, because that's not my goal or my passion.

Definitely reach beyond your current comfort zone with your affirmations. Keep your affirmations a step or two farther out than you're presently walking, but don't neutralize your affirmation by stating something that may be a remote possibility.

Start using affirmations to coach yourself to victory in all of life's efforts. Do it now!

ARE YOU FINISHED YET?

Maintaining a positive attitude is never truly completed. As long as we're breathing, we have the ability—the need—to learn and grow. Keep reading this book and any others that will help you. Remember, your attitude is your most priceless possession. I wish you a **super fantastic** journey in discovering the power and that lives within you.

God bless you.

KEITH HARRELL

Keith Harrell is a former IBM marketing executive and was one of their top training instructors with more than 13 years corporate experience. He has traveled around the world impacting the professional and personal lives of his clients. As a speaker, trainer, consultant, and author, Keith is highly recognized for his innovative and enlightening presentations. His high level of energy, enthusiasm, and powerful messages are exhilarating. Keith's unique and charismatic style of delivery compels participants to take a "fix-it" or "kick-it" approach toward desired changes in attitude, increased confidence and productivity. Keith is described by his clients as dynamic, humorous and motivational.

Keith's continuing search for knowledge and personal growth has led him to study the work habits of great leaders. Today, hew is president of Harrell & Associates, Ltd., in Atlanta, Georgia. Keith's affiliation with the National Speakers Association and American Society for Training

& Development continues to expand his knowledge and effectiveness.

The key to Keith's success is the time and effort he puts into researching his clients' business and industries. It's no wonder that many of Keith's engagements are repeat performances for groups such as IBM, Mattel, US Spring, and Eli Lilly. Keith and his staff recognize that a meeting or conference of any size is a big investment, and they are dedicated, committed and willing to team up with you to help make your next event the best ever.

When your plans demand a motivating keynote address, or an in-depth development seminar, let Keith's **Power, Passion and Purpose** assist your plans for achieving success.

OTHER PRODUCTS

Attitude is Everything T-shirt __ L __ XL $12.95
I Feel Super Fantastic T-shirt __ L __ XL 12.95
Attitude Quote Book #2 .... 10.00
Attitude Quote Posters (52 Posters 8.5 x 11) 20.00
Attitude is Everything Buttons (minimum order-10) 1.00
Attitude is Everything Audio Tape 12.00
Attitude is Everything Audio Tape Series (2 tapes) 24.00
Self-Confidence: The Key to Your Success (Audio) 12.00
Change: The Power for Growth (Audio) 12.00
Keith's New Book! Attitude is Everything® 20.00

Please add $5.00 Shipping & Handling

To order or for more information about Keith's products, speaking, training, or consulting services contact:

Harrell & Associates, Ltd.
3854 Sidestreet
Atlanta, GA 30341
(800) 451-3190 • Fax (770) 451-7232